The
Purpose Path

The
Purpose Path

A GUIDE TO PURSUING YOUR
AUTHENTIC LIFE'S WORK

Nicholas Pearce

ST. MARTIN'S
ESSENTIALS
New York

The Library of Congress Cataloging-in-Publication Data
is available upon request.

ISBN 978-1-250-18217-3 (hardcover)
ISBN 978-1-250-18218-0 (ebook)

Our books may be purchased in bulk for promotional,
educational, or business use. Please contact your local bookseller
or the Macmillan Corporate and Premium Sales
Department at 1-800-221-7945, extension 5442, or by email at
MacmillanSpecialMarkets@macmillan.com.

First Edition: April 2019

10 9 8 7 6 5 4 3 2 1

*To my childhood pastor,
the sainted Bishop Arthur M. Brazier,
the third pastor of the Apostolic Church of God
in Chicago, Illinois, who inspired my passion for
purposeful living, learning, and leading*

Contents

Foreword

I began wrestling with questions of purpose and vocation in my early twenties, some sixty years ago. Across forty years of writing, I've tried to share what I've learned about those questions with my readers, especially about the importance of letting our highest values guide the work we do and how we do it. After all, most of us will spend most of our waking hours working: the way we spend our days will end up being the way we spend our lives.

In a society that is forever preoccupied with the pursuit of more, it becomes all too easy to spend our lives chasing a cultural definition of success, to disconnect our working lives from "the better angels of our nature." But at age eighty, I know beyond doubt how important it is to seek a path more purposeful than one fixated on the pursuit of wealth, prestige, and power. Living what I call "an undivided life" means learning to listen more carefully for the still, small inner voice of vocation, recognizing our deep longing to join soul and role as closely as we can.

The invitation to journey toward an undivided life is an invitation to be made whole—which means to be vulnerable, to "wear our hearts on our sleeves" against all the cultural advice to the contrary. I'm ever grateful for people who inspire us to do exactly that through every kind of "weather" we encounter on the journey by walking their talk.

In his life, in his work, and in this book, Nicholas Pearce is one of those people. Like me, Nicholas was born on the bustling South Side of Chicago to hard-working parents who influenced the value he places on work and incubated in him an awareness of and a longing for the transcendent. Like me, he grew up going to church—but unlike me, he began wrestling with questions of vocation at the tender age of seven. As a leading business school professor and expert in the field of leadership and organizational behavior—and as a pastor serving the very church in which he was raised—Nicholas is a living, breathing example of an undivided life. For me, he is proof positive that vocation transcends career—and in this book, he shares some of his own experience with the tension between fidelity to the voice of one's vocation and the allure of conventional success.

Nicholas writes from the intersection of spirituality and work to communicate these essential truths with elegant simplicity and grounded authenticity. He writes to weary travelers on life's road who long to be free from the burden of fraudulence—the burden of betraying true self—and want more faithfully to express who they are *through* their livelihood, not in spite of it. At the same time, he speaks to younger people who are trying to summon the courage to start down the path with soul and role conjoined, to bring light, joy, and purpose to all they touch. He calls this "the purpose path," one marked by the bravery to align our deepest purposes with our daily words and actions.

In these pages, you'll meet influential leaders and everyday people—some who have found their way onto their own purpose paths, some who are still struggling with the disorientation and dissatisfaction that come from living a divided life. You'll read stories of clarity, conviction, and courage and see why connecting soul and role is so critical to good leadership. Nicholas deftly connects insights about purpose from the individual level to the organizational level, sharing stories of organizations that are thriving on their own purpose paths—as well as some that, while profitable, are losing their souls by ceaselessly engaging in activity that is divorced from the organization's reason for being.

Accepting the invitation to the purpose path demands that we acknowledge our complicity in willfully working at jobs and engaging in activities that flagrantly violate our values. When we live divided lives, each passing day gnaws at the fiber of our very being: I know because I've been there. I suspect that, like me, you've met many people who have grown numb to the hunger pangs of the soul that divided living can bring about. Inwardly, we know who we are and who we are meant to become, yet outwardly we ignore the voice of vocation and instead respond to the demands of others.

Even though we will never be able fully to harmonize our inward and outward realities, there comes a point at which the dissonance becomes too great a burden to bear, compelling us to give more weight on the imperatives of our hearts, liberating us to connect who we are with what we do. The need to align our daily work and our life's work becomes an inescapable yearning—not toward perfection, but toward wholeness.

If that's your yearning—or if you want that to be your yearning—this book is for you. Reading *The Purpose Path* is a wonderful place to begin or continue the exploration of what it means to connect your soul with your role and live an integrous, undivided life.

May the road rise to meet you on your journey.

—Parker J. Palmer, author of *On the Brink of Everything*, *Let Your Life Speak*, *A Hidden Wholeness*, and *The Courage to Teach*

Introduction

"The mass of men lead lives of quiet desperation."

So wrote Henry David Thoreau in his classic book *Walden*. Many millions of people anxiously look forward to the day when they can stop worrying about paying their mortgages, whittling down their credit card debt, and working in jobs they can't stand. They long to align their life's purpose with what they do every single day. After all, isn't that what every one of us wants—a life filled with purpose and meaning?

As we look to the future, we trust and hope and pray that one day we'll be able to live the kind of life that we dream of. But for most of us, the clock keeps ticking away the hours, days, and years, and we find ourselves no closer to the dream that, like a mirage, recedes from our grasp the closer we get to it. The reality is that fewer than 20 percent of Americans are working in their dream jobs. This suggests that for a significant part of most people's lives, their purpose and work are out of alignment. For a significant part of those people's lives, their life's work never gets accomplished in the course of their daily work. They ceaselessly strive down a path that, for them, seems to diverge from their true purpose.

In his book *Start with Why,* Simon Sinek explains the critical importance for organizations to identify and live their *why*—the purpose, cause, or belief that motivates and animates *what* they do and *how* they do it. According to Sinek, companies that know their why and live it—such as Southwest Airlines, Disney, and Apple—are the most successful, and they think, act, and communicate in accordance with their unique reason for being.

I am convinced that it is just as important for us as human beings to find our why—our purpose—and to create a life of significance deeply rooted in it. And we can't afford to wait another minute. As robots and artificial intelligence increasingly are deployed in businesses around the world, and as the global population continues to rise, there will quite possibly be more people chasing fewer jobs.

The time to act is not next week or next year. It is *now.*

The practice of *vocational courage*—boldly building a life of significance and not just importance—has been a key aim of my own life and has provided many an honest gut check for me along the winding path I have personally walked—and continue to walk—in an effort to live and lead with purpose. Vocational courage is not merely about job or career, fame or fortune, or even passion—it's about finding and pursuing your *true* purpose in life and about making sure your life's work is reflected through your daily work. In a world that's increasingly consumed with what people have, vocational courage is about connecting deeply with who you are and why you're here so that you can thrive in a society that constantly challenges the dignity and worth of our humanness.

As I explored the idea of vocational courage, I reflected on my own life and how I got to where I am today. As an undergraduate at Massachusetts Institute of Technology (MIT), I majored in chemical engineering, and that's the career path I initially expected to follow. However, for reasons that I will detail later in this book, I made a dramatic shift from that path to a new one that led me to discover a unique, multifaceted vocation for myself. In time, I built a career portfolio that was uniquely mine—serving as a professor, pastor, and executive consultant. While my work may appear to be comprised of three separate vocations that have little to do with one another, I always tell my students, clients, congregants, and colleagues that I do not have multiple vocations—I have a single vocation that motivates and encapsulates the work I am called to do on this earth. It is one vocation that plays out in a variety of ways on a variety of platforms—each supporting and intertwining with the others in interesting and powerful ways.

This book contains true stories about real people at

different stages in their lives—some whose lives have been enhanced by their vocational courage, and others who have come to regret their lack of it. These stories will help readers gain the self-awareness, clarity, and confidence to better understand their own life's purpose, commit to following a vocationally courageous path, and navigate the twists and turns of life with strength, wisdom, and courage.

Vocational courage is the boldness to faithfully pursue the fulfillment of one's distinctive purpose or life's work. It is about developing both the clarity and the commitment to make the difficult decisions necessary to align one's daily work with one's life's work. It is the fuel for living and leading on your own Purpose Path.

I have organized the content of this book into two parts.

In part 1—"The Five Questions"—I reveal the five questions that we must ask ourselves to explore our own purpose paths and create lives of significance. These questions derive from a distillation of my years of work in vocational courage and talks and conversations I've had with leaders, organizations, and everyday people all around the world. These key checkpoints for charting life's journey can help anyone assess their progress in pursuit of a more meaningful, vocationally courageous life.

These five questions are the heart and soul of this book:

- What is success?
- Who am I?

- Why am I here?
- Am I running the right race?
- Am I running the race well?

While exploring these questions, I take a deep dive into exactly what vocational courage is—and what it isn't. In addition, I explore the urgency for all of us to exhibit vocational courage in our lives. The hands on the clock move ever forward, and simply wishing, hoping, and thinking about how great it'd be if we dared to pursue the fulfillment of our life's work doesn't get us any closer to that elusive goal. Living a life of significance and purpose requires vocational courage, not just smart career planning. "Vocation" isn't just another word for "career"—it's about a calling, your life's work, and not just your job or work activities. Each of us is more than our job or chosen profession, and we don't have to wait until we reach a certain age to wrestle with the pursuit of our respective vocations. Exploring and living "into" your vocation is not to be deferred. Your vocation is not to be ignored. Your vocation is to be received and stewarded. It is a responsibility. It is both your joy and at the same time an ever-present burden you have been intentionally assigned. It is what gets you out of the bed in the morning. It is your reason for doing what you do—it is your raison d'être. This is not a book about how to pick a profession or choose a career. This is a book about how to pursue a path of purpose for your life and tapping into the strength you need to stay the course.

In part 2 of this book—"Putting Vocational Courage to Work"—I show how you can apply the principles of vocational courage in your own life and in the lives of others. While a vocation is a gift to be received, it is also a journey to be walked. And any vocation worth living for comes with inconvenience. In order to do this well, we have to have the courage to make difficult decisions about our future. We can be clear on what our life's work is, but not have the commitment to faithfully fulfill it. That's why I call *true* success "faithfulness." Success cannot be defined by the extent to which you achieve someone else's measurement of impact. Instead, success must be defined by the extent to which you have been consistently faithful and focused on courageously walking your own purpose path.

Ultimately, living on the purpose path is accepting the invitation to a life of vocational courage. It involves gaining clarity about who you are and who you have been created to be—an understanding of why you are on the planet. It also involves relentlessly committing yourself to courageously living out your unique *why* every single day. It is more than understanding what you love to do, what you are good at doing, or even what you wish you could do—it is refusing to settle for doing anything less than what you *must* do because you were specifically created to do it. It is saying yes to completing your life's assignment no matter the cost, complexity, or inconvenience.

This is a book for . . .

. . . teens and twentysomethings who are trying to

figure out how to purposefully and intentionally orient themselves as they make the transition from high school or college to life as a working adult.

... thirtysomethings who didn't have this courageous conversation in their twenties and are now beginning to feel a sense of restlessness, frustration, and being stuck in their chosen careers while knowing deep within that they were truly made for more. It's even for those who had the conversation in their twenties but need to revisit it as life has changed.

... forty- and fiftysomethings who are beginning to look in the rearview mirror and evaluate the net impact of their lives and longing to live lives of purpose and significance while they can still pivot at their professional prime.

... sixty- and seventysomethings who are mentoring and coaching the next generation, while grappling with the same kinds of issues as the forty- and fiftysomethings. They are even more anxious to experience meaning and purpose in their lives as they begin to consider cementing their own legacy.

... parents who want to give their children a gift that has the power to change their lives for the better.

... leaders who want to connect with their people and teams by investing in their personal and professional well-being.

... churches and other communities of faith that want to spark a spiritual conversation with their people about the purpose and meaning of their lives.

We owe it to ourselves to find meaning and take deep pride in what we do in the service of others. We owe it to ourselves to build lives of meaning and significance that inspire us to wake up every morning and make a difference.

That's *real* courage.

My sincere hope is that this book will change your life—and the lives of the other people with whom you share it and its ideas—dramatically and for the better. I look forward to meeting you and celebrating your own stories of vocational courage. I look forward to hearing about how you discovered the gift of vocation and then summoned the courage to stay the course on your own purpose path when you needed it most.

PART I

The Five Questions

*The greatest gift is not being afraid
to question.* —RUBY DEE

believe the practice of *vocational courage*—boldly building a life of significance and not just importance—is imperative for each and every one of us. Doing so is not just so we feel a sense of happiness or fulfillment, but because it's our responsibility and privilege to follow the path of purpose for which we have been uniquely created. Vocational courage is not simply about the job you select or the career you pursue, or about gaining fame or fortune, or even about finding your passion in life.

At its very heart, vocational courage is about finding and pursuing your *true* purpose in life, and about making sure your life's work is reflected in your daily work. In this first part of the book, I offer and explore in great detail the five questions I have found most effective in coaching people of all ages as they seek to discover their true purpose in life and chart a course for leading a vocationally courageous life of purpose. These five questions do not come out of thin air. I have developed them over a period of years of wrestling with vocational courage in my own life and in working with people from different walks of life, from everyday people to high-powered executives and organizations of all sizes in every sector.

As I noted in the Introduction, the five questions I explore are:

- What is success?
- Who am I?
- Why am I here?
- Am I running the right race?
- Am I running the race well?

1

What Is Success?

We are prone to judge success by the index of our salaries or the size of our automobiles, rather than by the quality of our service and relationship to humanity.

—THE REVEREND DR. MARTIN LUTHER KING, JR.

In high school, Annie Little's most important value was *freedom,* which she defined at the time as physical and financial independence from her parents. Annie's family dynamic was not a particularly pleasant one for her when growing up, and Annie was committed to doing everything she possibly could to avoid having to rely on her parents after she graduated from college. While still in high school, Annie decided that the best way to achieve her goal was to become a lawyer. Says Annie about the reasoning behind this choice, "I grew up with several friends whose parents are lawyers, and they all had nice houses, fun vacations, cool clothes, and their lawyer parents had interesting stories."

In short, lawyers were successful people, and Annie wanted to be successful, too.

So Annie put her focus on doing the things required to become a lawyer. She earned stellar grades in high school and was accepted by Northwestern University, where she majored in religion and psychology. As she neared her senior year of college, Annie scored well on the LSAT—the standardized test used by most American law schools to help make admission decisions—and she was admitted to the University of Minnesota Law School. For Annie, law school wasn't an afterthought—a fallback position—it was her first choice and her guarantee of future success.

Soon after graduating from law school, Annie was offered a position at a law firm in Philadelphia. Over the years, Annie worked her way up from an entry-level position to the partnership track. She was skilled at her job, and it seemed to suit her well. However, cracks were beginning to appear in the foundation of Annie's pathway to success, and they soon began to trip her up.

Annie was becoming increasingly frustrated that her requests for pay raises based on her performance and the profitability of the firm were being ignored. Perhaps even worse, however, was that the monotony of the work she was doing was beginning to bother her. If this was what success was supposed to look like, she thought, then it sure didn't look as glorious as she'd expected.

At about this time, Annie was offered a position with a different firm, which would allow her to expand into other areas of law while providing her with a significant salary boost. For Annie, this was a no-brainer, and she quickly accepted the position.

She was back on the fast track to success.

Until she wasn't. "I became bored and frustrated in a matter of months," says Annie. "No sooner had I learned everyone's name in my new firm than I started looking for new jobs."

Annie interviewed with numerous law firms—from boutique to regional to international—and with companies seeking in-house counsel, but she received no offers. She began to feel trapped by the decision she had made so many years earlier, when she was just a teenager. "On paper," she says, "I had everything I ever wanted. Or at least what I thought I wanted—six-figure salary, successful career, supportive husband, beautiful house, luxurious vacations, and legitimate net worth. Yet it wasn't enough." Annie's reflection revealed that she had reached her goal of becoming what most people would call successful, but she says that she "had failed in finding work that was meaningful" to her.

In other words, Annie was *successful*, but she didn't feel like a *success*.

Realizing that the professional life she had chosen was no longer aligned with her values, Annie sought the services of a life coach to help bring clarity to what had become a very confusing situation. In less than two weeks, she had her answer. Says Annie, "The values and priorities of my younger self were not the same as those of a thirtysomething professional."

While independence to a teenage Annie meant not having to rely on her parents any longer, independence for a thirtysomething Annie meant:

> *starting a family, not working full-time while raising babies, being able to travel for longer than a week at a time, knowing with certainty that I wouldn't have to work on any given weekend, being able to live wherever I want regardless of whether or not I'm licensed to work there.*

Annie's definition of her most-important value— *freedom*—had changed, and it was now in direct conflict with her chosen career—the practice of law. The moment Annie realized that this was the source of her unhappiness, she knew that something would have to change if she was ever to truly become a success and not just successful.

After considering a variety of different options—starting her own business, going back to graduate school, pursuing an entirely different kind of legal job—Annie left lawyering behind once and for all, and instead became a life coach. In this way, she could achieve the kind of freedom that her thirtysomething self craved, while helping others find *their* paths in life—making a real difference in the lives of her clients.

And perhaps most gratifying for Annie is that this new brand of freedom has given her the time she needs to make a difference in the life of her daughter. Says Annie:

I didn't want her to know me as an attorney. I didn't want to teach her it's okay to trade her happiness for a career she hates just because she's good at it or earns a hefty salary or doesn't know what else to do. I wanted her to know she gets to decide what success looks like for her.

We all want to experience success in our lives—to achieve the goals we set for ourselves, to make enough money to live comfortably, to surround ourselves with real friends and a loving family that bring us warmth and joy, and to make a lasting difference in the world around us.

But what exactly *is* success, and why do so many of us have such a hard time being *a success* instead of just successful?

The Nature of Success

Each of us has our own idea of what success is; there's no easy one-size-fits-all definition that can be applied to every person. Consider the cases of Brenda Barnes and Indra Nooyi.

Brenda Barnes, who passed away in 2017, was for a time

one of the most powerful women in business. Starting as a business manager at Wilson Sporting Goods, Barnes worked her way up through the executive ranks as vice president of marketing at Frito-Lay, various top executive positions within PepsiCo, and then in 1996, president and chief executive officer (CEO) of Pepsi-Cola North America— the largest beverage division of a huge global organization with $7.7 billion in annual revenues.

When Barnes resigned her position running Pepsi-Cola North America after just a year and a half to spend more time with her elementary-school-age children and her husband, she triggered a firestorm in the media. Some applauded her for putting her family first, while others felt she had done the cause of increasing the number of women in the boardroom and in top executive spots an extreme disservice.

But through it all, Brenda Barnes held firmly to her own definition of success, that at least for some portion of her life, she needed to put the focus on her family instead of on her career. Speaking of the internal struggle she went through to reach this level of clarity, Barnes said:

Every time you would miss a child's birthday, or a school concert or a parent-teacher discussion, you'd feel the tug. You wished you were there.... I'm not leaving because they need more of me, but because I need more of them. I suppose a lot of chief executives can find a way to balance work and family, but I couldn't figure out how to do it with 100 percent commitment to the company—in a way that would give me a role in my children's life.[1]

On her own timetable and on her own terms, Barnes did eventually return to the corporate world. She served on the boards of *The New York Times*, Avon, Staples, Sears, and Lucasfilm. When her children were in high school, Barnes decided that she could dedicate even more time to business. She became president and chief operating officer (COO) of Sara Lee in 2004 and was named chairman and CEO in 2005, serving there until she suffered a stroke in 2010.

Another former PepsiCo top executive has drawn attention for pursuing her own unique definition of success— one that stands in stark contrast to the one that Brenda Barnes defined for herself.

Indra Nooyi started her career at PepsiCo in 1994 and worked her way up to CFO in 2001. Nooyi was named president and CEO of the global food and beverage giant in 2006, added chairman to her title in 2007, and stepped down as CEO in 2018. Nooyi, who throughout her tenure at the helm of PepsiCo appeared on annual lists of the most powerful businesspeople and women in the world, earned a reputation for her intense work ethic and devotion to PepsiCo. While earning a master's degree at Yale, she worked the 12:00 A.M. to 5:00 A.M. shift as a receptionist, and freely admits that she routinely worked until 12:00 A.M. at PepsiCo.

In 2014, Indra Nooyi triggered her own media firestorm when she said in an interview:

> *I don't think women can have it all. I just don't think so. We pretend we have it all. We pretend we can have it all. My husband and I have been married for thirty-four years. And we have two daughters. And every day you have to make a decision about whether you are going to be a wife or a mother, in fact many times during the day you have to make those decisions. . . . We plan our lives meticulously so we can be decent parents. But if you ask our daughters, I'm not sure they will say that I've been a good mom.*[2]

Some observers were shocked that this powerful woman executive would put the needs of her company above the needs of her family. But it is not anyone's place to decide what success means to Indra Nooyi except for Indra Nooyi. And during her time at PepsiCo, she clearly decided that success for her, at least at that leg of her life's journey, involved putting PepsiCo first to ensure its future growth, profitability, and long-term success. In pivoting away from the helm of PepsiCo, she illustrated the importance of understanding the season of life in which you find yourself and how being a success takes on new dimensions as one's purpose path unfolds.

In my experience, I have found that few people actually take the time to figure out what success is for them. Many mistakenly assume it's universally defined, as though everyone on the planet has the same aspirations and keeps score in life in the same way. Many others operate on the flawed assumption that someone else has the right to impose his or her personal view of success upon them.

While some people think success means attaining the goals that have been set for them by others—whether by their families, their managers, the media, or societal norms and expectations—others think success means following in the steps of those successful people who preceded them. Still others are blinded by the intoxicating sparkle of fame and fortune as the measure of true success.

Back in 2014, Strayer University and Ipsos, a global market research firm, conducted a survey to find out what success means to Americans. Fully 90 percent of those surveyed said that success is more about happiness than power, money, or fame. (In fact, only one in five respondents felt that monetary wealth is what defines success.) In addition, 67 percent felt that success means achieving personal goals, while 60 percent believed that success is loving what you do for a living.[3]

The problem is that relatively few people have the courage to look deep within themselves to get to the heart of what *true* success means to and *for* them. Granted, there are many people on the planet for whom success lies almost exclusively in making sure that their families have enough food to eat, clean water to drink, and adequate shelter. But for those of us who have the opportunity to choose what we want to be when we grow up, it behooves us to choose our life's path in a way that allows us to pursue and accomplish our unique definition of success, rooted in our sense of purpose and core values. This isn't just for the well-heeled Ivy Leaguers among us. This is something that everyday people can—and should—do.

For many of us, it's a struggle to clarify how we define success for our lives, not to mention how we pursue it. And when we don't, the consequences for our careers—and our lives—can be devastating.

One of those consequences comes in terms of how we show up to work every day. Gallup has tracked employee engagement—the extent to which people are emotionally committed to their work and their employers—for years. Unfortunately, the news is not good. According to the Gallup polling organization, only 33 percent—one-third—of employees in the United States are engaged at work, and just 13 percent worldwide are.[4] This widespread disengagement leads to lower productivity, decreased work quality, and lower job satisfaction.[5]

When you think about it, this is an alarming statistic. Fully two-thirds of the American workforce does not feel a deep connection to the work they do; they are simply going through the motions, day in and day out.

One of my deepest desires in writing this book is to provoke people to come off the autopilot mode that allows them to somewhat mindlessly navigate through their lives, and to pause for a moment, and say to themselves, "Hmmm . . . I didn't think of what my life could be like if I lived every day on purpose." If people think through the questions I pose in this book, and if they engage in more intentional moments of self-reflection, then my firm belief is that this will both encourage and challenge them to live lives that are more vocationally courageous and ultimately more meaningful and impactful.

True vocational courage comes from defining what success is for us, based on our own unique purpose and core values, and then making the difficult decisions necessary to wholeheartedly pursue it. True vocational courage does not come from following someone else's definition of success, nor from having others define success for us. It's not about trying to achieve the kind of success that your parents pressured you to achieve because they couldn't achieve it themselves. And it's not about trying to achieve the kind of success that your boss defines for you at work, or your spouse/partner, friends, and other influencers define for you in your daily life outside the office.

It's about knowing your own values and then allowing those values to guide what success means to and for you—and you only.

It's about being willing to honestly explore and answer the question "How do you keep score in life?"

Many people choose to keep score in life by how many material possessions they can accumulate. They keep score by how many trophies are in their capitalistic display case—sprawling homes, luxury automobiles, designer clothes, fine jewelry, and expansive bank accounts. It is important to note that these things are not inherently bad. But the truth about the relentless pursuit of this definition of success is that such success is fleeting, depreciable, and corruptible—in fact, it can be taken away in the blink of an eye.

To be a true success, we need to adopt a definition that is more intrinsic, more internal, and more eternal—a definition that is designed to support our faithful pursuit of why we are here. Defining success in this way allows us to measure our clarity, commitment, and consistency in pursuing our life's work as the end and the means—not some goal that someone else has set for us.

So, the first step toward becoming an authentic success is making sure you have clarity regarding what success means to you and what you have to do to achieve it.

Can You Be Successful Without Being a Success?

I have a good friend who spent the early days of his career in the tech industry. He was a business executive at a Fortune 500 company in the Silicon Valley, and he had all the trappings of success: he had a brand-name college degree, he was a key player in a growing business unit in a growing company, and he was making bucketsful of money.

But after a few years of going one hundred miles an hour in that direction of being successful, his life smashed into a concrete wall. He realized that, while he was doing all the "right" things to be successful in terms of his career and his financial well-being, he was empty on the inside. He got into drugs to medicate the pain he was feeling, and his career, family, and life began to slide into a very deep abyss.

He was successful but not a success.

Fortunately, this executive could see that the definition of success he was chasing was eventually going to destroy his family and kill him. While he was successful by most anyone's definition of success, his life was not trending that way; he was on an extremely self-destructive path. So he walked away from the high-powered career as a tech executive and he stepped back from his life to reorient himself and redefine what success meant to him.

Instead of returning to the tech sector as an executive, which many people would consider the most tempting choice, he began mentoring and advising other leaders who were trying to start organizations in the tech space. He coached entrepreneurs and became a venture capitalist, funding promising tech start-ups. He completely switched gears, from being a high-powered Silicon Valley marketing executive to starting what many would consider an encore career at a relatively young age. For him, though, it wasn't an encore career. It was what his new definition of success meant for him, and it allowed him to be more present and a better person for his wife, for his kids, and for himself.

And, as he would readily admit, it quite literally saved his life.

He's happier, healthier, and far more satisfied with his life now than he ever was in his previous career. Instead of walking along a path of what success means to someone else, he has courageously decided to walk his own purpose path, leading to greater professional impact and personal well-being.

It's always others—coworkers, family members, random onlookers, or even society at large—who seem most concerned with evaluating whether or not you are "officially" successful.

You have a lot of money—you're successful.

You have a beautiful family—you're successful.

You have a nice car and wear nice clothes—you're successful.

You have an important title—you're successful.

You're powerful and influential and have high status—you're successful.

You accomplished what someone said you should—you're successful.

But did you accomplish what you were uniquely *supposed* to do with *your* life? If not, the question is not whether you're successful. You can be successful at the *wrong* things. You can be successful and at the same time *not* be an authentic success. You can appear to be successful by an outward evaluation of your accomplishments—the trappings of your success—but not be a success when you evaluate yourself inwardly, according to your sense of self, your purpose, and your vocation. So the question is this: "Are you content with being *successful* but not being a *success*?" I believe we should encourage and extol the virtue of being a success—that is, being significant and not just looking important by others' standards.

We naturally think of someone who is important as being successful because his or her name is known; when people see this person they applaud, and when the person enters a room, people stand. That's certainly the mark of someone who is powerful and successful in a certain way, but being a success is a different phenomenon. While these things don't have to be mutually exclusive, true success is really about *being* more than *having*—being vocationally courageous with or without the fancy career and the related accoutrements.

There was a time not long ago when some people equated the strength of your faith with how healthy you were or how much stuff you had. If you had enough faith, you wouldn't get sick. If you had enough faith, you'd have enough money.

How could you possibly worship a God who supplies endlessly, and not have what you need if you really have the faith? Then the Great Recession hit. Then some of the same people who espoused that teaching started seeing their retirement savings erode. Real life started to happen. Then this whole correlation between one's faith and one's outward trappings started to be seen as shoddy: it was a shoddy, broken, invalid claim that held neither theological nor practical merit. Hardship has a way of maturing people, and it's something all of us must go through in our lives. The alleged correlation between the strength of one's faith in God and the accumulation of outward trappings has been debunked. It's not a real thing, and many people are now focusing much more on who you are inside and how you are growing in your faith and living out your faith, as well as demonstrating it and teasing apart the external façade from the real you.

Today, many more people—especially those in the millennial generation—are asking, "What's the meaning behind what we're doing? What's the purpose? How is what I'm doing making the world a better place? Is there something more transcendent that I can be doing with my life and time?" This kind of questioning is extremely important; it gets us back to the essence of what matters most. If you keep score only by what you can see, then success doesn't have anything to do with what lives on beyond you, except for that which is material, which can be stolen, lost, devalued, and corrupted.

There's a Reason Why We're Here

If you believe that the purpose of man is to be born, to live, and to die—and that's it—then all we have is here and now. All we have are our toys and our trophies, the things we can see, touch, taste, and smell. But if you adopt a perspective that there's more to life than what is seen, then there's more to achieve than what can be physically sensed and experienced. There is a higher purpose beyond just surviving and multiplying.

There is something about us that desires to live on. There's something about us as human beings that longs to have a sense of legacy, a sense that we're leaving something behind that will endure beyond our physical life. That then suggests that we are wired to want to achieve far beyond the span of our lives. Worthy goals are not just ones we can experience the fruit of while we live. If that's the case, then how we define success and the pursuit of our life's work should be no different.

To me, success is the daily commitment to being faithful to doing what you've been created to do. So then success is defined by your Maker—by the Creator not by the creation. If you make something, you don't give it the opportunity to define what its reason for existence is. You made it with some intent for a particular function, some intent for a specific, predestined purpose. You already had an idea of why you wanted to make it, and you, as the creator of this thing, can measure whether or not it fulfills what you designed it to do.

But advances in technology threaten to disconnect us from our work and the sense of purpose we derive from doing it. One of my colleagues, Rob Wolcott, wrote an article in *Harvard Business Review* about how advances in automation promise to change work, purpose, and human meaning. Rob suggests in his article that as technology becomes more widely available, "more of us will face the question, 'When technology can do nearly anything, what should I do, and why?'"[6] I will dig more deeply into the intersection of technology and purpose in the next chapter.

There's going to be pain on this journey called life; alignment between your definition of success and your unique purpose does not protect you from the pain. In fact, it almost guarantees it. It's not just about how happy you feel, or how warm and fuzzy you are around others. Sometimes you have a tough row to hoe, but there is a deep contentment in knowing that you're doing what you're supposed to be doing with your life. Despite the ups and downs and the unpleasant moments, you can still have the gift of deep and abiding contentment, encouraging you to stay the course. Even amid the pain, there is a peace that you can't quite describe that comes from knowing that you are in the place where you belong—not just in a comfortable career.

PROFILE IN COURAGE: *Oprah Winfrey*

Few stories highlight the power of the purpose path like the story of American media pioneer, entrepreneur, and global philanthropist Oprah Winfrey, dubbed the Queen of Daytime TV. Born into poverty on her grandmother's farm in rural Kosciusko, Mississippi, Winfrey confesses that despite her stellar successes and international fame, she didn't always know who she'd become, but "it was just very clear . . . from an early age who I wouldn't be." A black girl born in the American South in 1954 faced seemingly insurmountable odds to rise above the racism that ruled the day. Despite the odds she faced, she clung to a clear definition of success that transcended the circumstances in which she found herself. As she watched her grandmother work, boiling clothes in a big black cast-iron pot, something came over Winfrey. She heard a "still, small voice inside [of her] . . . which said, 'This will not be your life. Your life will be more than hanging clothes on a line.'" She credits the "certainty of that divine assurance" with getting her through some of the toughest, most traumatic moments of her childhood. Oprah's definition of success was borne out of a deep desire to inspire others to exceed their own limitations—a desire that was rooted in her own lived experience. Though she never fathomed her life's work would result in becoming a globally recognized personality with a platform to reach the world, her pursuit of success was driven by a sense of calling. Says Winfrey, "I believe there's a calling for all of us. I know that every human being has value and purpose. The real work of our lives is to become aware. And awakened. To answer the call."[7]

The word "career" comes from the French, denoting a racetrack. For many of us, our careers feel like we are on a hamster wheel, going around and around in circles, going literally nowhere fast. If career achievement is how we measure success, then we are resigned to defining success as crossing the finish line first in a race in which we go in circles—a race in which there is no net forward movement and we finish exactly where we started, exhausted and discouraged.

There has to be a better way to think about how we spend our time, how we spend our days on this earth. That's where this concept of *vocation* comes to the forefront—this notion of one's calling or life's work.

Success isn't about winning a race against your neighbor to see who amasses the most money or power. Success is measured by the impact you have on individual lives, doing the right thing, setting a positive example, being the best you can be, and doing all the good you can for all the people you can in all the ways you can for as long as you can. Success is changing the world around you in ways large and small, such that even if your name is not remembered, your impact will outlive you.

I often ask my students and the leaders that I have the opportunity to serve, "Will you still do something with your life that's worthy of applause, even if no applause is given? Will you become someone who is a success, even if there's no recognition? Is your drive for recognition or for vocational fulfillment?"

So, what do you do when you realize you're not being a success—when you aren't doing what your Maker designed you to do?

You ask yourself, "Am I running the right race?" Then you pick a new target and you set new goals that will allow you to be successful at being a success. You make being a success the goal. We all have so many activities in our lives—things that take control of our calendars and ultimately threaten to take control of us. We need to pause and think about who we are being and who we are becoming, not just what we're doing.

If it's true that we need to focus on who we are being and who we are becoming, then *being* a success should be more important than *doing* things that make us look successful. We are much more than what we do and what we have. We are human beings, after all, not human doings.

2

Who Am I?

Discovering vocation does not mean scrambling toward some prize just beyond my reach but accepting the treasure of true self I already possess. Vocation does not come from a voice "out there" calling me to be something I am not. It comes from a voice "in here" calling me to be the person I was born to be, to fulfill the original selfhood given me at birth by God.

—THOMAS MERTON

The human brain is a marvelous and tremendously complex system—approximately eighty-six billion neurons (nerve cells) communicating with one another via chemical neurotransmitters that travel across microscopic gaps known as synapses. It is within these three pounds or so of complexity that humans developed *consciousness*—"the fact of awareness by the mind of itself and the world."[1] According to science writer Anil Ananthaswamy, researchers have revealed that:

. . . the self is not some monolithic thing sitting in the brain or outside the brain. It's actually a whole set of neuro-processes, which need to work in concert for us to have a sense that we have a being, that we are an entity to whom things are happening and have a perspective on the world.[2]

Without a doubt, consciousness is one of the greatest gifts we humans have received from our Creator, not least of which because it enables us to answer the question "Who am I?" It is instrumental in determining our social identities—the groups (e.g., faith tradition, race, ethnicity, tribal affiliation, socioeconomic class, profession, first language, generation) to which we belong and how we interact with others—both in and out of those groups.

For some, answering the question "Who am I?" is straightforward and simple. For others, however, answering this question is . . . complicated, to say the least.

Barack H. Obama was born in Honolulu, Hawaii, in 1961. His father, Barack Obama, Sr., was a black African born in Nyang'oma Kogelo, a village in western Kenya, about twenty miles distant from the shores of Lake Victoria, near Kenya's border with Uganda. His mother, Stanley Ann Dunham, was white—born in Wichita, Kansas. Barack's parents were married in 1961—six months before Barack was born—and he and his mother lived in Hawaii while Barack's father pursued undergraduate studies at the

University of Hawaii and then graduate studies at Harvard. Because the scholarship he received from Harvard did not include sufficient funds to bring his family along with him, Barack Sr. left his wife and young son behind in Hawaii.

Hawaii is considered to be the most racially diverse state in the Union. According to the US Census, Hawaii is 37.8 percent Asian, 25.7 percent white, 10.2 percent Native Hawaiian and other Pacific Islander, 2.2 percent black, and a surprisingly large number of Hawaiian residents count two or more races in their heritage: 23.8 percent.[3] Perhaps because Barack grew up amid such pronounced ethnic diversity, his own mixed heritage was not a big deal to him growing up. In his book *Dreams from My Father,* he explains, "That my father looked nothing like the people around me—that he was black as pitch, my mother white as milk—barely registered in my mind."[4] Barack's parents divorced in 1964—his father returning to Kenya, where he became a government economist and was killed in a car crash in 1982.

In 1965, Barack's mother married Lolo Soetoro, a student at the University of Hawaii who returned to his native Indonesia in 1966, and Barack and his mother followed in 1967. Barack lived in Jakarta until 1971, when he returned to Hawaii to attend school. After graduating from high school in Hawaii, Barack first enrolled in Occidental College in Los Angeles, and then Columbia in New York, where he earned his degree in political science and international relations. He went on to attend Harvard Law School, where he earned his JD degree in 1991.

Life went on for Barack, but he was haunted by the ghost of the father he barely knew and the African roots that had been severed when his parents divorced. He was very familiar with his mother's side of the family: he moved in with his mother's parents when he returned to Hawaii, and he heard tales of his ancestors, who had come to America from Scotland and England in hopes of a better life, who had fought for the Union in the Civil War, and even one ancestor who was full-blooded Cherokee—but his father's side of the family, and his African heritage, was shrouded in mystery.

"Who am I?" is surely a question Barack asked himself over and over again as he grew from his teen years into adulthood.

That is, until 1987, when he flew to Nairobi, Kenya, to make the journey to his father's homestead in Nyang'oma Kogelo, where Barack would have the opportunity to reconnect with his African roots and fill the void that had dug its way into this part of his life. In *Dreams from My Father*, Barack asks:

> Would this trip to Kenya finally fill that emptiness? The folks back in Chicago thought so. It'll be just like Roots. . . . A pilgrimage, Asante had called it. For them, as for me, Africa had become an idea more than an actual place, a new promised land, full of ancient

traditions and sweeping vistas, noble struggles and talking drums. With the benefit of distance, we engaged Africa in a selective embrace—the same sort of embrace I'd once offered the Old Man. What would happen once I relinquished that distance? It was nice to believe that the truth would somehow set me free. But what if I was wrong?[5]

Soon after landing at Jomo Kenyatta International Airport in Nairobi, Barack began to immerse himself in his lost homeland and to gain a sense of where he came from and who he was. When Barack realized his luggage had not arrived in Nairobi along with his flight, a security guard offered to summon a British Airways employee to help. The employee—Miss Omoro—took one look at Barack and asked if he was by chance related to Dr. Obama. When Barack responded that Dr. Obama was his father, Miss Omoro explained that his father and her family were close friends, that Dr. Obama had visited her home many times. Already, there was something very different about this place—the land of his father and his father's ancestors. Says Barack:

For the first time in my life, I felt the comfort, the firmness of identity that a name might provide, how it could carry an entire history in other people's memories, so that they might nod and say know-

ingly, "Oh, you are so and so's son." No one here in Kenya would ask how to spell my name, or mangle it with an unfamiliar tongue. My name belonged and so I belonged, drawn into a web of relationships, alliances, and grudges that I did not yet understand.[6]

During the course of his journey to his father's village, Barack took in the sights, tastes, sounds, smells, and feelings of Africa. He met relatives he never knew he had, he glimpsed endless savannah vistas, vast herds of zebras, wildebeest, and gazelles, and he saw groups of Masai women— with earlobes stretched long—walking to the marketplace. He heard stories about his bighearted father and how those whom his father helped turned their backs on him when his fortunes changed for the worse. And he learned about the fierce family infighting over the modest inheritance Barack's father left behind when he died. Barack soaked up every moment, feeling like he belonged to this land, to this people, to this earth. Barack says:

It wasn't simply joy I felt in each of these moments. Rather, it was a sense that everything I was doing, every touch and breath and word, carried the full weight of my life; that a circle was beginning to close, so that I might finally recognize myself as I was, here, now, in one place.[7]

Barack was home, in the land of his father and his father's fathers. And he was finally able to more fully answer the question "Who am I?"

The Nature of Identity

If you look up the word "identity" in a dictionary, you'll find a definition along the lines of "The fact of being who or what a person or thing is," or "The characteristics determining who or what a person or thing is."[8] While these definitions are certainly correct, I consider identity to be *one's own sense of who he or she is*. Identity is very deeply *who* you are—not who someone else thinks you are or wants you to be. Your *identity* is how you define yourself, while your *identification* is how others define you. How you identify yourself does not necessarily need to match how other people identify you. While it is true that our families and communities play an important role in shaping how we see ourselves, ultimately, how others attempt to define you is no substitute for how you answer the question "Who am I?" for yourself.

When it comes to the question "Who am I?" I adopt the perspective of theologians who have, down through the centuries, looked at humankind as body, soul, and spirit.

Considering what makes us human beings, many people point to the anatomical, physiological, and biochemical aspects of our humanity, including the DNA constituting the human genome. Others focus on human beings' intellectual capacity and socioemotional cognition, including the ability to imagine, create, critically reason, and maintain self-awareness.

But what makes us distinctly human is not just our physical bodies, nor is it our physical or intellectual human capacities, because machines are able to do some of those very same things. And as artificial intelligence and automation continue to advance, our capacity to think is no longer uniquely human, because there are computers and artificial intelligences that can think faster and more efficiently than we can. In many cases, machines can outthink and outremember human beings, and their capabilities will only grow in the years to come. My colleague Rob Wolcott has written extensively on this subject, and he predicts that artificial intelligences will become faster and better than human beings in almost every arena of human endeavor.

There is a physical self and also a psychological self, both of which are greatly affected by how we have been raised and by other formative influences in our environment. Each of us has been brought up in different environments, with different combinations of family relationships, teachers, friends, and others who have had a hand in our development. But I contend that having a body and having an intellect are not what make us uniquely human; it is having a spiritual self that truly humanizes us.

I believe that defining what it means to be human by

what we are able to do with our bodies or our brains is limiting. To be sure, our bodies are an important dimension of our humanity, but I point to a much deeper sense of what it means to be human—that we are spiritual beings contained in wrappers of human flesh. Consequently, we must grapple with that spiritual reality if we are to answer, "Who am I?" "Why am I here?" or any of the other questions that follow in the pages of this book.

I look at the spirit as the flame inside each of us that influences our thinking and our behavior. The Scriptures explain that the spirit can not only influence but even control the mind. Paul the Apostle writes in Romans 12:2:

> *And do not be conformed to this world, but be transformed by the renewing of your mind, that you may prove what is that good and acceptable and perfect will of God.*[9]

This verse speaks to the formation of a spiritual identity that takes place by the transformation of the mind. This spiritual formation is accomplished by the renewing of one's mind, which suggests, then, that the mind definitely informs and influences the formation of identity. When spiritual transformation takes place, it is not mindless, thoughtless, or purely emotional, as many suppose. It is indeed mind over matter. That renewal not only has purely spiritual implications, but also important practical implications for what we do with our bodies. Our deeper spiritual identity should dictate what we do with our bodies, not to mention what we do with our time and talent.

That's what makes us uniquely human and distinctly different from artificial intelligences. It's not just that we have capacity to do things with our bodies, but the governance of our minds and what we do with our bodies is a spiritual matter that artificial intelligences do not and cannot encompass.

To me, the discovery and formation of our true identity has everything to do with our relationship with the One who made us—God.

Discovering Your True Identity

The idea of knowing who you are and thus what you were designed for is inextricably linked to your relationship with the One who made you. To the extent that God is the Creator of all, God is responsible for the creation and maintenance of human life—indeed, for *all* life.

Though this book is not intended to deeply focus on questions of the creation of the universe, it stands to reason that the vast, complex system of this universe and all that is in it had to be caused by something or someone. Philosophers and theologians, including Saint Thomas Aquinas, have written extensively on the fact that there must be a self-existent, self-explanatory, "uncaused cause" that is responsible for the universe and everything that is in it—regardless of one's preferred explanation of how creation came into existence.

For me, God is the first cause.

Based on the premise that God causes life, then the source of identity comes from one's spiritual lineage and parentage. Just as one's physical identity is informed by one's DNA, which is informed by biological lineage, true identity is a matter of one's spiritual DNA. The shaping and forming of one's true identity—one's best self-identity—is rooted in a relationship with God.

While many of us have been gifted with great parents, teachers, and others whose influences were instrumental in our maturation, many of us have not. Ultimately, a relationship with God helps us to discover who we are and who we were always meant to become.

How Others Influence Our Identity

The people around us—friends, family, coworkers, our managers, and so on—have the ability to impact and help shape our identity. Sometimes others help shape us in good ways and sometimes in less-productive ways. Sometimes people try to shape us into becoming who they want us to be, or into who they wish they themselves could be. That means we have to be mindful of whether we're being formed into a clone of someone else or whether someone is actually contributing to the development of *our own* best self. As an old adage of apocryphal origin states, it is best to be yourself, because everyone else is already taken.

PROFILE IN COURAGE: *Carmita Semaan*

One leader with whom I've had the opportunity to collaborate, who exemplifies the power of understanding how one's identity shapes and influences one's life's work is Carmita Semaan. A Birmingham, Alabama, native, Carmita was trained as a chemical engineer and started her career at Procter & Gamble. After finishing business school at Northwestern University's Kellogg School of Management, she briefly pivoted into global product management before she recognized that she was made for more. She made the transition from corporate life into public education and was haunted by the lack of leaders of color across the sector. When she launched the Surge Institute in 2014, she emptied her bank accounts and drew on a significant portion of her retirement savings because she saw a problem she knew that she had to solve: she was distressed at the dearth of leadership of color at the decision-making tables within education reform, which had implications for children of all stripes across the country. She recognized that as a leader of color, she had been called to lead the movement that would benefit generations of kids and leaders just like herself. The Surge movement is sweeping the nation and impacting the education sector one city at a time. Carmita's story proves that vocational courage can often come at significant personal expense. Like Carmita, your life's work may be disguised as a problem that you are uniquely well suited to solve—a problem that you cannot not tackle. Sometimes you just have to trust yourself and take the leap.

Nevertheless, a core part of my own identity, at least professionally as a pastor, was shaped by how I saw my childhood pastor, Bishop Arthur M. Brazier, carry out the work of pastoral ministry. Seeing his intense commitment to the Lord and seeing how he loved people and led them with integrity gave me a sense of what *my* pastoral identity might look like, having had a great model in him. Models and people who are investing in our formation are very, very important. But we have to be clear that every model that we see may not be showing us what we should aspire to be. They could be showing us what not to be or what not to do. There are some great human beings—role models perhaps—who are great at being *them,* and while there are some things we could learn from them and apply to our own lives, we have to resist the urge to try to become that person. That's an important distinction.

We often hear about role models and people we want to be like when we grow up, and so we often face the temptation to mimic everything that they do, not recognizing that they have a different assignment. They have a different reason for being here that is ultimately attached to them. Just unique as their DNA is, their assignment is unique. While there are some things we can learn from and even adopt, becoming them—expressly patterning our lives after them—may not get us the same type of success that they have enjoyed, because the success they've enjoyed is tied to their faithful living out of who *they* are, and what they are called to. Carrying out someone else's assignment is not going to get you the same fulfillment or the same results, because that's not *your* assignment.

The formative influence of others in shaping identity is undeniable. But when do we follow the guidance of others, and how do we know when to set it aside? It's all a matter of how it resonates with you spiritually. There are people who will have very kind things to say, but those things have to resonate at a spiritual level. When the guidance you receive resonates spiritually, it should not surprise you, even though it may have been the first time you heard it. It may have been a thought that never occurred to you consciously, but at a spiritual level, it should not feel strange. In fact, you might respond with an almost otherworldly sense of, "Yes, of course this is true. This may not be something that I've consciously thought about. This may not be something that even sounds good to me, because it may require some sacrifice or some difficulty, but something in my spirit tells me that this is aligned." There's a lightbulb moment, so to speak—not in terms of new knowledge, but in the confirmation of knowledge that was already in you but was perhaps unconsciously hidden to you.

The Johari window—a tool developed by psychologists Harrington Ingham and Joseph Luft—is a useful tool for better understanding this kind of insight into who we are. The window is square, divided into four different quadrants. On one axis is what is known to others and what is

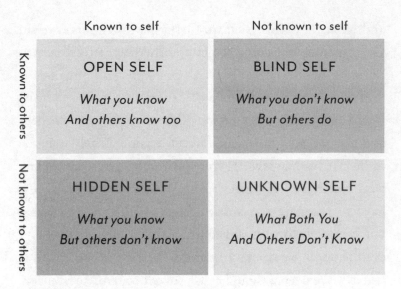

The Johari Window

unknown to others. On the other axis is what is known to self and what is unknown to self. Based on these inputs, the four quadrants describe insights that are:

- known to self and others ("open" self)
- known to self, but not to others ("hidden" self)
- not known to self, but known to others ("blind" self)
- not known to both self and others ("unknown" self)

In other words, when other people are speaking into your life, there may be things about you that they know or have observed, and that, even though you may not consciously know them about yourself, once they become known, they immediately click. They fit. They're not strange to you at all.

You may have blind spots; we all do. I firmly believe that God uses other people to help in our formation by providing valuable perspective in areas that may not be consciously known to us. But keep in mind that these people are not always positive role models—men and women who are good and just and honest and who deserve our honor. God oftentimes uses flawed human beings to accomplish supernatural objectives. They serve as sterling examples of the kinds of people we should not model ourselves after nor become.

How We Hide Our True Identity

People get hired into new jobs, and they're understandably very excited about the opportunity. But sometimes they'll be there for a week or two and then they suddenly realize that the workplace doesn't fit. They're not aligned with the workplace, or the workplace is not aligned with them. People ask themselves, "Am I in the right place?"

Many people find themselves in workplaces that are antithetical, if not hostile, to their identities, and so they engage in what sociologist Erving Goffman terms *covering*— downplaying an identity that may be known to others. New York University law professor Kenji Yoshino has built upon this work to examine how people fail to disclose parts of themselves in order to avoid the perceived penalty that would come from being identified as a member of that stigmatized group. It explains how people who are in the minority, whether in terms of race, gender, religion, or even disability status, are often pressured to conform with the dominant group and the social costs that come with minimizing who we authentically are.

One way that people cover is through appearance. For example, a Muslim woman may have the strong cultural prescription to wear a hijab, but because her Muslim identity is under threat in her workplace, she may opt not to wear one so that she will not be identifiable as a Muslim and be negatively targeted or discriminated against.

Covering can affect how you speak up for other people at work as well. We see this with women in the workplace, who might say, "Because being a woman is not the celebrated or dominant identity here, I had to work and scratch and scrape to get whatever I've got. So I'm not going to support other women; they need to make it all on their own, like I did." Former U.S. secretary of state Madeleine Albright once said, "There's a special place in hell for women who don't help other women." When women will not help one another, that's a way of attempting to cover the fact that they too are women.

Covering can also impact how people choose to associate or affiliate with others. An undocumented immigrant employee might say, "I don't want to hang out with my undocumented immigrant colleague, because I'll be identified as one of *them*. I don't want to be identified as one of them, even though I *am* one of them. So, I'm going to distance myself from others from my own community." Some millennials are facing this same identity threat with companies that have millennial business resource groups. Because the millennial generation is widely stereotyped as entitled, disloyal, impatient, and self-absorbed, many millennials decide to opt out of these groups that were designed for them, because they do not want to be associated with those negative stereotypes. They will not join the millennial business resource group lest they be lumped in with all "those millennials."

Our identities are under constant threat in the workplace, so how you respond to these threats—especially if you are from an underrepresented group—can be a critical determinant of your well-being and authentic self-expression.

The Changing Nature of Identity

Identity evolves, and I believe we all have multiple social identities—not a psychological, split-identity disorder, but simply that we are multiple things all at once. We are spouse/partner, parent, child, sibling, employee, team member, community member, church member, and much more. Not only that, but as time marches on, our identities can shift. In fact, I would argue that one of the things that can cause distress as people mature is the inability to embrace new identities and new expressions of who they are. There are people whose marriages begin to fray once their kids are out of the house, because while they started out as a husband and as a wife, their primary identities at home shifted to those of mother and father, and the husband/wife identities were put on the back burner. So now that the kids are gone, the mother/father identity takes on a different expression, and they don't know how to adjust.

While parts of our identity may shift and evolve over time, what is most essential to who we are at the core should not change. It is a matter of deeper self-awareness and self-discovery. From my point of view, spiritually speaking, that discovery is rooted in a relationship with God, because God is unchanging. The conversation you have around vocational courage is about being clear on what is unchanging, so that those activities you undertake from day to day—which will change—will always be aligned with your core identity.

Identities will change. You will go through different stages in your life, and parts of your identity will evolve. But who you are at the core remains the same. Your *why* is dictated by your *who,* and your *what* is dictated by your *why.* All of that is rooted in stability of your core identity.

Character and Its Relationship to Identity

Think of character in terms of one's core operating principles or core values. I think about character in terms of how we go about living out our identity. What are the operating principles that characterize how we live our life?

Core values often grow out of how one sees oneself. Who I believe myself to be will then dictate my values. That's why, from a spiritual perspective, pastorally, I do not believe that the Gospel is about surface-level behavior modification or merely imprinting a particular code of morality. There's a difference between having faith in God and being a moral person. Trying to get people to consistently live with and act with strong character—absent a strong sense of identity—is like trying to fit a round peg into a square hole. When you try to get people to either engage in behavior changes, which is the *what*, or engage in moral thinking, which is around *character*—but you don't really address their identities—they always revert to what seems most authentic to their identities.

I believe that one's true identity drives behavior. If you view yourself as CEO material, then you should be operating in an executive-like way. You're carrying yourself with a degree of executive presence, and you are operating with values that inspire confidence and respect in you as a leader before you have the title, because your identity drives your character. It drives your decision-making. It drives your activities. It drives what you do in life. Identity precedes values, and it precedes behaviors.

A core part of identity is purpose, which is an expression of your why. Why am I here? Purpose ought to drive everything that follows. Purpose dictates values. Purpose drives behaviors, just as in an organizational culture a company's purpose drives its practices. An organization's purpose dictates its core principles and therefore its routines and activities. The same thing is true with people.

Consider that the core values, character, personae, and value systems of founders can have a tremendous impact on organizations themselves. Much has been said about the dysfunctional culture in the early years of ride-sharing company Uber as a direct result of the core values and character of its cofounder and CEO Travis Kalanick (who was forced to step down in June 2017 after a shareholder revolt resulting from a string of sexual harassment claims against the company).

Companies reflect their founders. Then later—when the founders move on—they reflect their executive teams. The word "character" has its origins in the Greek word for a stamping tool—the imprinting of a stamp of one's image. If you think about character as imprinting, what makes two companies in the same sector different is not simply their strategies or their products and services—those can easily be mimicked. What makes them different is not their *what*. It's their *why* and their *how*. They end up attracting different kinds of people to work in each company, people that are aligned with those cultures. Character flows throughout the organization.

There is an exponential ripple effect that comes from having clarity and consistency around who we are and why we are here. The improvements in operational excellence in terms of doing what we do better can come later. It is essential to put first things first and keep the main thing the main thing. Having clarity and consistency around who we are and why we are here allows us to do just that.

Some companies do a particularly good job of answering the question "Who are we as a company?" and they are able to explain it to customers and to the general public. Ben & Jerry's, 3M, and Southwest Airlines are just a few of these companies. They're not only selling products or services, they are serving people, and that is clearly shown in their policies, their procedures, their corporate values, and everything they do.

Essential Steps in the Process of Self-Discovery

Let's return for a moment to the question and the title of this chapter—"Who am I?" When I ask that question, I don't believe it's necessary for you to have an exhaustive answer, but staying tuned to your own self is a necessary step in being able to demonstrate vocational courage. Why? Because if you're not paying attention to the question of who you are, you will allow yourself to be distracted by how *others* define who you are—especially if others define you positively.

Many people started their careers with some idea of what kind of work they were meant to do, but they made a sacrifice to take a job that didn't fit their purpose in life in order to pay off their student loans, support their families, or for some other reason. Later, they know this career was never really right for them, and it's no surprise, since this was not the purpose for which their Maker designed them. They might say, "This is not core to who I am and it's not authentic to me. The values that I'm being asked to live out every day are not aligned with my own, but I'm going to do the job anyway—I need the money."

Invariably these people were promoted, and their increased income became too much to turn down. They were put on a high-potentials list or other external marker that proclaimed, "This is who you are to us," and they were soon sucked up in the outward identification of who they could become to someone else. This was of course very intoxicating to them, and ultimately it dragged them off course.

We have to be able to answer the questions, "Who am I?" and "What is most core to me?" But we also have to make a commitment to keeping these questions front and center in our vision of where we are going in our lives. Whether you're a millennial who is trying to launch a new business, a thirty- or forty- or fiftysomething who is making a major career or life pivot, or you're approaching retirement age and looking to rewire for the next decades of your life, ask, "What does this stage of my life look like? What does my legacy look like? How do I do what is vocationally courageous at this stage?" and "How do I invest in the next generation and their vocational courage?"

These are the questions to keep asking yourself as you navigate the pivot points you will inevitably encounter during the course of your career—and life.

When we're getting ready to graduate from high school or college, most of us don't really know what we are going to do or what we are going to be. Unfortunately, few young people have a clue. If someone had this conversation with me about vocational courage—in terms of linking what I do with who I am—when I was coming out of high school, I probably would not have majored in chemical engineering. I always looked at vocation as job or career, not as my life's work. No one was having a conversation with me about life's work. It was all about, "What are you good at?" and "What do you want to be when you grow up?" The better questions would have been, "Who are you?" and "What course of academic preparation will best equip you to do what you are created to do?"

It's a conversation I wish someone had had with me, but it seems that relatively few people around me ever had that conversation with themselves.

Remember, the ability to have this conversation is something of a luxury. There are some people around the world who have a sense of self that's very strong, and they find great meaning in their work, even though it does not make an obvious large-scale impact on society. They don't have the luxury of getting to pick how they're going to enact that sense of self every day to change the world. They have to do what they have to do to put food on the table and put a roof over their family's head and to survive.

When I look back in my own family, generations ago, this sort of conversation would have been a nonstarter. I'm grateful to my parents, whose investment in me and whose raising of me put me in a position where I could ask this question. I am grateful that I had the support to courageously do so. Now I have the opportunity to inspire and challenge thousands of other people to ask it of themselves.

The main question is one of identity, and identity is inextricably linked to purpose. Who you are dictates why you are here. Who you are dictates what you're going to do and how you're going to do it. This is foundational. It is necessary. It is quintessential to aligning your daily work with your life's work.

This book is an invitation to come off of the autopilot mode of merely doing and really engage at a deeper level of who you are. Based on that deeper engagement, are you doing what you should be doing, what you uniquely are well suited or even called to be doing? I believe form follows function. So understanding who you are at the most essential level and how you view your identity and how you are formed from that identity will help shape the answer to what you should be doing. Without clarity about who you are, you will never know whether what you're doing is aligned with who you have been made to be.

3

Why Am I Here?

There are two great days in a person's life—the day we are born and the day we discover why.

—WILLIAM BARCLAY

In 1942, Viktor Frankl—along with his parents and Tilly, his wife of less than a year—were rounded up by the Nazis and sent to the Theresienstadt ghetto, a concentration camp about thirty-five miles north of Prague in what is now the Czech Republic. There his father died of pneumonia. Two years later, in 1944, Frankl, his wife, and his mother were sent to Auschwitz, where his mother was immediately killed by the Nazis. His wife, Tilly, was transferred to Bergen-Belsen, where she was murdered, and Frankl was sent first to the Kaufering and then to the Türkheim concentration camps, where he remained until Türkheim was liberated by Allied troops in 1945.

During his time in the Nazi concentration camps, Viktor Frankl witnessed the very worst of humanity—and the very best. He and his fellow prisoners were mercilessly kicked, pummeled with rifle butts, whipped, and beaten by their captors for such innocent transgressions as falling out of step while marching, stumbling to the ground, or tripping on a rock. And, of course, many were murdered in the gas chambers or killed with a gunshot to the head or electrocuted by an electric fence.

But Viktor also saw his fellow prisoners choose to go hungry by giving their food ration for the day to someone whom they felt needed it more than they did.

One has to wonder if Frankl and the many others in the German concentration camps asked themselves the question "Why am I here?" What had they done to deserve such a fate? And did their lives still have meaning and purpose? Viktor Frankl believed that everyone's life has meaning—that each of us has a reason for being—and it is up to us to discover this meaning and live it. In his book *Man's Search for Meaning*, Frankl wrote about the revelation he had in the death camps:

> *I told my comrades (who lay motionless, although occasionally a sigh could be heard) that human life, under any circumstances, never ceases to have a meaning, and that this infinite meaning of life includes suffering and dying, privation and death. I asked the poor creatures who listened to me attentively in the darkness of the hut to face up to the seriousness of our*

position. They must not lose hope but should keep their courage in the certainty that the hopelessness of our struggle did not detract from its dignity and its meaning. I said that someone looks down on each of us in difficult hours—a friend, a wife, somebody alive or dead, or a God—and he would not expect us to disappoint him. He would hope to find us suffering proudly—not miserably—knowing how to die.[1]

Everyone in those barracks had a choice to make: whether or not they were going to attach meaning to their suffering. This decision was a difficult one to make in light of the questions that everyone had: "Why me? Why do I have to be the one to suffer? Why am I the one who is going to die?"

"Why am I here?"

Of course, there was no answer to these questions. The only way for these men and women to survive their brutal day-to-day existence was to rethink their circumstances. Instead of asking why they were caught in these circumstances, they had to ask an entirely different question: "What does life want from me?" Said Frankl:

Questions about the meaning of life can never be answered by sweeping statements. "Life" does not mean something vague, but something very real and concrete, just as life's tasks are also very real and concrete.

They form man's destiny, which is different and unique for each individual. No man and no destiny can be compared with any other man or any other destiny.[2]

Viktor Frankl did survive the death camps, and in doing so he helped countless others understand the meaning of their own existence—the answer to the question "Why am I here?" True thinking is not driven by answers, but by our questions. Every situation, every decision, every circumstance we go through calls for us to candidly consider the reason why we exist on the earth, to embrace it, and to live it fully in everything we do.

Why Are We Here?

I firmly believe that every single person on this planet has a purpose and a reason for being. I've worked with thousands of emerging and established leaders around the world, in every sector. What's surprising to me, however, is that the vast majority of them are able to articulate their organizations' reasons for being with far greater clarity and conviction than they can articulate their own. This is alarming but not surprising.

The question "Why are we here?"—the meaning of life— has been wrestled with by philosophers, scientists, and theologians since the dawn of humanity. Some psychologists would say that purpose is derived from your ability to master challenging tasks, and perhaps chief among those is to avoid death—to continue to exist. And there are biologists who postulate that the purpose of life is merely to replicate one's DNA and perpetuate one's gene pool. In an interview, James Watson—who codiscovered the structure of DNA with Francis Crick, and won a Nobel Prize for his efforts—said, "Well I don't think we're *for* anything. We're just products of evolution."[3]

I do not agree with this assessment.

According to the teachings of Aristotle, the highest good for human beings is something he called *eudaimonia,* which has been translated from the Greek as "well-being," or "human flourishing." Other philosophers have discussed modest pleasures, happiness, personal fulfillment, and similar concepts—linking them to what we are here on this earth to achieve—our *purpose.*

I personally believe that purpose has a more transcendent dimension to it, that everything was created with a purpose in mind. And not just we as human beings, but the entire environment in which we live—the earth and the sky and the plants and animals, large, small, and everything in between. There is purpose in all of this, even though that purpose may not appear important at a surface level.

The deeper you dig, the more you understand the way the plants and the animals and the air and the surroundings interact with one another in a systematic, interdependent way. It's a very intelligently designed system, and that is difficult to deny. So, upon deeper examination, each of us can discover what our purpose is. I don't believe it is simply to maximize our happiness and satisfaction. I don't believe it is to accumulate as much stuff as we can get. Some would say: to get all you can, and can all you get. I don't think our purpose is that superficial.

I think Aristotle took a step in the right direction when he talked about the highest good for its own sake. But Aristotle's term *eudaimonia* became linked with the idea of well-being, which to many people is synonymous with satisfaction and happiness. This avenue, I believe, becomes increasingly mundane. I think the idea of purpose, or the idea of meaning, is tied to God, to worshipping God, and in so doing to not only serve God but to serve humanity. That's why we're here.

We're More Than Just Flesh and Bones

For centuries, theologians have wrestled with the question of why we're here. The *Westminster Shorter Catechism,* written between 1646 and 1647, talks about purpose in this way: "Man's chief end is to glorify God, and to enjoy him forever."[4] So, when I think about purpose, to me there's always a transcendent dimension to it.

Theologians are divided into two major camps when it comes to the question of why we are here.

One group believes that we are simply body plus soul—an idea labeled *bipartite*. John Calvin is notable among those who have espoused the idea that man is body and soul—material and immaterial. The other group espouses the idea of man as *tripartite*—body, soul, and spirit. In this view, which has its roots in the Old Testament, soul and spirit are two separate entities. Soul is the seat of emotion—the intellect, our ability to make sense of the world and sense of ourselves. Spirit is that God-conscious space that has control over body and soul. As such, it influences the activity and behavior of body and soul.

Regardless of whether someone subscribes to a particular theistic view—bipartite, tripartite, or whatever—the fact that we are more than our physical matter is something that most of us would agree to. There is more to us than just our physical, material existence.

Unfortunately, many descriptions of the meaning of life point to a purely material existence, and regardless of whether one subscribes to a belief in the afterlife, it's a fact that in this life there's more to us than just flesh and bones. There is intellect. There is emotion. There is conscience. There is self-consciousness. There is desire. There is will. So I believe that with an acknowledgment of that deeper, more essential aspect of humanity comes the responsibility, even the privilege, to discover what each person's purpose truly is.

Many people will say, they are spiritual, but not religious. This is true even among millennials in mainline Protestant Christian denominations, where there has been a rise in what are known as the *nones*—people who don't identify with any particular religious group. According to a study conducted by the Pew Research Center, the number of adults who count themselves among the nones rose from 36.6 million in 2007 to 55.8 million in 2014—comprising 23 percent of the US adult population, and 35 percent of US millennials.[5] They have spiritual peace absent any form of organized religion.

I think Aristotle's idea of *eudaimonia* points to this notion of human flourishing, and I think the idea of purpose as being connected to the well-being and welfare of *others* in the world around us is important. Jeremy Bentham, an eighteenth-century English philosopher of this utilitarian perspective, suggested:

> *Create all the happiness you are able to create; remove all the misery you are able to remove. Every day will allow you,—will invite you to add something to the pleasure of others,—or to diminish something of their pains. And for every grain of enjoyment you sow in the bosom of another, you shall find a harvest in your own bosom,—while every sorrow which you pluck out from the thoughts and feelings of a fellow creature shall be replaced by beautiful flowers of peace and joy in the sanctuary of your soul.*[6]

This is a very functional, utilitarian perspective. I believe that the humanist perspective that we only exist for our own pleasure is limited. Creating lasting value for other individuals, or for populations, is critically important for us as human beings.

PROFILE IN COURAGE:
Dr. Gardner C. Taylor

Widely regarded as the Dean of Black Preachers and the poet laureate of the twentieth-century American pulpit, the Reverend Dr. Gardner Calvin Taylor retired as the pastor of Brooklyn's Concord Baptist Church of Christ in 1990 after an acclaimed forty-two-year tenure. Despite the fact that his father, the Reverend Washington Monroe Taylor, was a pastor in his native Baton Rouge, young Gardner did not want to follow in his father's footsteps to the pulpit—he instead wanted to be a criminal lawyer. That all changed one devastating afternoon while he was a student at Leland College. He served as a chauffeur to the college's president, and while driving for him one day, another car swerved across the highway and led Gardner to crash his car into a ditch to avoid a collision. In the aftermath, one man lay dying and another lay severely injured. As a black young man in rural Louisiana—where lynching black people was quite common—Taylor feared for his life in the wake of the accident. Yet, when the investigation yielded two witnesses who testified that Taylor was not at fault for the fatal accident, he knew that God was real. Even though he'd been admitted to the University of Michigan Law School, Taylor reversed course, acknowledging a call to the Christian ministry and enrolling in Oberlin's Graduate School of Theology in 1937. Through this traumatic experience, Taylor was led to embrace who and what he was called to be all along. Why would God allow such an episode to play out in his life or ours? Sometimes the traumatic experiences of our lives can shake us into a meaningful awareness of what our life's work truly is.

However, not everyone's life's work will involve creating a tremendous impact on the entire world for generations to come, so it's important not to entangle purpose with scale. Just because someone's life has had an impact on a greater number of people, does not make their life more purposeful. That perspective would reduce purpose and meaning to only what we can see terrestrially. I deeply believe that each of us has a specific, transcendent assignment that we have been given and for which we are uniquely well suited and even called. That's the idea of vocation.

Connecting with others is an essential part of being human. Research shows that people who have fewer connections with others experience all sorts of negative outcomes. Their physical health declines, their mental health declines, and their performance in careers and jobs declines. It all goes downhill. The more connections people have with others, however, the better their health and overall well-being. Having meaningful social connections decreases the likelihood of clinical depression, heart disease, and early mortality, all while increasing happiness and life satisfaction.

So, you don't have to focus on answering the question "What's the big thing I'm going to do to have an impact on the world?" By forging strong, meaningful relationships and connections with the people around you—family, friends, neighbors, work associates, members of your community— you *are* having an impact on the world. The example we set in our own lives speaks volumes, and when people see you doing good things for others, many will want to follow your example.

As you consider your purpose, your reason for being, it's important to have clarity around what is uniquely yours to do. I'm a firm believer that not all good work is necessarily good for you. There are many important issues to be tackled and critical problems to be solved for the good of humanity: environmental protection and sustainability, public education reform, biomedical breakthroughs. Nevertheless, there is some good work that is not *yours* to do. Just because it isn't yours doesn't mean it is somehow less noble or less worthy. So instead of saying in a blanket way that you will "do good," find that work that is uniquely yours—the work for which you were made and to which you have been specifically assigned in order to bless others.

Improving the Quality of Life for Others

Your life's work is going to take place within the context of community; even monks have monasteries where they live out their calling with others. To accomplish your purpose, I believe, requires you to interact with some other person, or population of people, in some meaningful way. It's not just a transactional, army-of-one kind of work. Purpose is most often discovered and lived out in community.

So how can we have some bearing on this quality of life for others?

We see problems in society that frustrate us, and we want to solve them. We see problems in someone's everyday life, and we want to make his or her life better. We see opportunities to enhance human flourishing all around us.

We try to build a world where everyone has access to food to eat, where everyone has access to clean water, where everyone has access to medical care. Some people are advocating at a policy level. Some people are building the technical solutions. Some people are financing those solutions. Some people are playing lower-profile, behind-the-scenes roles. No matter the part one plays in the cast, we all have the opportunity to be a part of doing something that blesses our neighbors, if only we look for it. Sometimes, it's just a matter of adopting the right perspective to see how one seemingly insignificant activity can make a significant impact.

I'm reminded of the story of three bricklayers who were in the midst of constructing a new building. Someone walked up and asked the first bricklayer, "Why are you here?" The first bricklayer responded, "I'm just here to do what they ask me to do and get a paycheck." The second bricklayer was asked the same question by the passerby, and he responded, "I'm just here to build this wall." Finally, when the third bricklayer was asked why he was there, he responded—looking up into the heavens—"I'm here to build a cathedral."

The same task. The same activity. But an infinitely different perspective about it.

To have some bearing on others' quality of life, it's not necessary to take a big, glamorous role in a high-powered global organization. Instead, deeply reexamine the work that you're doing, look at the impact that it's having on others, and find meaning in it. If we adopt the right perspective, most of us will find that we have the opportunity to love what we do because of the good it adds to the world, however obscure.

I think about the people at the university who clean the chalkboard after I teach, or who make sure that my computer is connected properly to the projector in my classroom, or who serve the food in the cafeteria—people who might be considered "support staff," often fading into the background unseen, unnoticed, and unfortunately underappreciated. But they have very meaningful roles in our university. If you bother to take the time to ask them about what they're doing, they can tell you how what they do connects to the bigger picture—a meaningful purpose. Undertaking what might be considered menial behind-the-scenes tasks may not seem like a high-status, "successful" career for anyone, but it's truly meaningful work for many of the people who do it.

That's why it's important to never overlook people who have a different socioeconomic status, or a different level of educational attainment, or who are employed in a blue-collar service profession. Just because they're not earning a certain amount of money does not mean their work is any less meaningful or that they are of any less worth or purposefulness as human beings. Our worth is not defined by what we do or what we have, but by who we are.

Every human being has inherent value. I believe that every human being is created in the image of God, so, as a bearer of God's image, *you* have worth. You have value. It is not for us to determine who has value and who doesn't in the common societal distinction between the haves and the have-nots. These categories don't correlate to the substance of one's purpose. Every human life has meaning. Every single one of us has a purpose for which we have been made and has the ability to discover it, an ability that is not linked to one's social or financial status. There are people who are billionaires who are not functioning with a clear sense of purpose, and people who clean those billionaires' homes who have a deep sense of purpose that drives them every day.

We Each Have a Unique Reason for Being

Every faith tradition and every school of philosophical thought from Aristotle to Plato to Confucius on down—Western or Eastern—has wrestled with and developed its own response when it comes to the questions, "Why are we here? What is the meaning of life?" and "Does humanity have purpose?" People have been wrestling with these questions since the beginning of time, and we will continue to do so for as long as there are humans to ask them.

Understanding *who* you are, from an identity perspective, then leads to your understanding of *why* you are here. *Who* you are and *why* you are, are connected. If you view your identity as a child of God, then your reason for being is connected to that identity. If you believe that God does not exist, then all you have is the here and now, and you perceive your reason for living as having no transcendent spiritual dimension.

PROFILE IN COURAGE: *A. J. Velasco*

Discovering your reason for being isn't easy or automatic—it's often an iterative process full of trial and error. A. J. Velasco was one of my students at the Kellogg School of Management who wrestled with vocational courage and charting out a path that would prepare him for his unique life's work. He had a background in investment banking, but he knew that after business school, that was not where he wanted to return. He received an internship opportunity in Silicon Valley as a strategic business development associate and loved it—and his employer loved him so much that he was approached with an offer to stay in Silicon Valley and not return to complete his Kellogg degree. After wrestling with the financial, academic, and personal consequences and implications, he decided to stay in Silicon Valley for two years. However, at the end of the two productive and rewarding years, he withdrew from that company because he recognized that completing business school was a necessary step for his life—even though he didn't know what the next step would look like after graduating. He also knew that his girlfriend lived in Chicago and that returning to business school would allow him to marry the woman of his dreams. Now he's one of our recent alums with a smaller remote role at the same Silicon Valley start-up and a wonderful wife, Julia. A. J. has opted to take some significant professional leaps but has come to recognize that life is far more than one's profession. He's still wrestling with the question of what impact he desires to make in the world, but he's using his current role as a skill-builder as he clarifies what his life's work might look like.

As you consider your vocation and how it relates to your reason for being, it's important to understand that your passion is not an integral part of this equation. To find your true vocation—what you are truly meant to do with your life—you can't simply pick what you're most passionate about and pursue it. Purpose is much more than passion.

This book is not about just finding your passion, and it is not about doing what you love, although your purpose *can* be something you are passionate about, and it *can* be something you love. But I believe living your purpose leads to loving what you do, even if at times it causes pain. Being driven by purpose leads us to activities and undertakings, not vice versa. In other words, the *why* must drive the *what*.

Vocation is not about personal satisfaction. This idea is being peddled to people, and people are getting confused as a result. They think, "If it doesn't feel good, this cannot possibly be my purpose. If I'm not enjoying myself, this cannot be purposeful. I've got to go find my passion. I've got to go find what I enjoy and do what makes me happy."

With all due respect to the people who are pushing happiness as life's chief end: I think everyone should have the right to lead a happy life, but there is not always a direct relationship between purpose and feeling good. In fact, living purposefully quite often leads us to adversity that we could avoid if only we abandoned purposeful living. Lighting up the pleasure and reward centers in our brains by doing whatever makes us feel good in order to experience happiness cannot be the reason why we're on the planet. Happiness is a by-product—a derivative side effect—of living purposefully, but not the ultimate goal of life itself.

My Own Reason for Being

I grew up on the South Side of Chicago, where I was blessed to have a supportive family, school, and church community. After graduating from high school, I enrolled at MIT as an undergraduate student, majoring in chemical engineering. During my sophomore year, I conducted with my classmates a lab experiment on zebra fish—testing the resilience of this creature that shares 70 percent of its genetic code with humans.

This experiment made me begin to wonder how to build strong leaders and strong organizations that could demonstrate resilience amid adverse conditions. And because I cared far more about the people in organizations than I did about a life filled with experiments on fish and other animals, I made the decision to embark on the study of the people side of organizations.

I worked with a professor at MIT's Sloan School of Management, helping to create a new minor in management for undergraduate students. My professor, Thomas Kochan suggested that I should consider doing organizational research and get my PhD. Hoping to increase my impact in the field, I became a doctoral student at the Kellogg School of Management at Northwestern University, studying all kinds of organizations. While I didn't yet know what I would do with my PhD, I knew the things I was learning would be important in my life, whatever it was I ultimately decided to do.

But that wasn't the only path I chose.

Church has been an important part of my life for longer than I can remember. I was called to ministry when I was just seven years old, and when I was sixteen, I had a conversation with my pastor about wanting to make a difference through the church. That started the ball rolling. A few months before I graduated from Kellogg with my PhD, I was appointed assistant pastor of Chicago's Apostolic Church of God, at the time the youngest in that position since the fifteen-thousand-member church was founded in 1932.

I eventually built a career hybrid that was uniquely mine—serving as a professor, pastor, and organizational consultant. On the surface, this hybrid appears to be three separate vocations, but for me it is a single vocation that allows me to do the work that I believe I am uniquely called to do. It is one vocation that plays out on multiple platforms.

The common fate for most of us is to spend the majority of our lives laboring at work, often in jobs that don't fulfill us. But why is it that some people seem to operate in their careers with an *uncommon ease*? And why do some retired executives who are widely lauded as "successful" reflect back on their careers with a profound sense of emptiness? The answer is simple: vocational courage—or the lack thereof.

In the oft-quoted words of Dr. Benjamin Elijah Mays, former president of Morehouse College, "[T]he tragedy of life doesn't lie in not reaching your goal. The tragedy lies in having no goal to reach. . . . Not failure, but low aim is sin."

I think about my purpose as glorifying God in all that I do. While that may appear self-evident given my pastoral work, my first ministry is my family. Family is critically important. There is no amount of social impact that I can make beyond the walls of my home that will outweigh underinvesting in the people and relationships inside my home. Neglecting one's marriage or children in order to pursue impact outside of the home often backfires with lasting, intergenerational consequences. This is especially true when it comes to pastoral ministry, as 1 Timothy 3:4–5 admonishes pastors that if they cannot take care of their own family well, they should not be trying to take care of the family of God by leading in the church. I have seen many people forsake home in favor of external impact, when perhaps the biggest impact you can most directly make is in your own house. Taking care of my family is as important to God as anything I can do outside of my home to bless other people.

Beyond my house, living out my purpose involves holding on to a deep sense of calling—not only to the pulpit, but also to the classroom and to the marketplace. When you are on the journey of purposeful living, you will find yourself being led into opportunities to advance your life's work that you could not create or even imagine for yourself. For me, this involves remaining sensitive to the leading of the Holy Spirit and staying open to the formative guidance of a community of people around me whose voices I trust. As we saw with the Johari window, we all have blind spots, but other people can help you fill in the blanks. And when they fill in those blanks, it won't strike you as strange. It may be new information, cognitively, but spiritually you will say to yourself, "Oh, right—I knew that already deep down within," even though you'd never actually articulated it before.

I love what Parker Palmer says in his book *Let Your Life Speak*:

> *Some journeys are direct, and some are circuitous; some are heroic, and some are fearful and muddled. But every journey, honestly undertaken, stands a chance of taking us toward the place where our deep gladness meets the world's deep need.*[7]

So finding those needs that you are uniquely well suited to address—globally, locally, or both—becomes the critical path. Choosing my own path was not easy; in fact, it was filled with uncertainty. As I was wrapping up my PhD at Kellogg, I wrestled with what I should do next. Obvious options were few.

The most straightforward path was to become a tenure-track professor, but I knew that to become a tenure-track professor, I would have to walk away from pastoral ministry for a period, and doing so was not at all consistent with my purpose. I knew that at a certain level, my academic work was to be in service of my pastoral ministry, not to serve as a distraction from it—even for a season. I really wrestled with that decision for years.

In general, doctoral advisors have a strong self-interest in replicating themselves, which means having their students become professors like they are. I knew that motive, generally speaking, and so I struggled with how to have this crucial conversation with my advisors to get the advice I needed. One of my advisors knew I was a pastor and affirmed that identity. And as I wrestled with next steps after my PhD program, we talked about the importance of trying to carve out a unique path, one that supported my identity.

Being both a pastor and business-school professor is not a common combination, and as I struggled with the fear and apprehension that came with moving into uncertain territory, my advisor, Katherine Phillips lovingly but sternly said:

Nicholas, you know who you are. Stop acting like you don't know who you are. You know what you're supposed to do with your life. Let's figure out a way to create a blend of professional activities that allows you to do what you know you are supposed to do with your life based on who you are. You know who you are. I know who you are. Let's not ignore it.

That ultimately led to the creation of my professorship and the work I do at the church as an assistant pastor happening concurrently, not in different seasons of life.

Asking Our Maker, "Why Am I Here?"

Any creation derives its existence from its creator, and in the mind of the creator is the function of the creation. So, if you subscribe to the concept that we are created and governed by God, then understanding God's intention—and God's design for human life and your life in particular—is a natural next step. A relationship with God, first, prompts the journey of greater self-discovery.

If you have an issue with your car or truck, who do you call? You call the manufacturer of the car or truck, and you ask them these questions: "What is this piece for? What did you make this for? What was in your mind when you made this?" Why? Because they designed and created and built your vehicle, they know everything there is to know about it.

We were created by God, in His image, so who better than Him to ask these questions? It makes complete sense to seek the mind and the heart and the intention of God, who created human beings, the earth, the seas, the universe, and everything beyond it, and everything within it, across time—operating outside of time, but in time. It makes sense to ask God such questions, not only including "Why am I here?" but also "How do I fit in the broader context of the world you have created at this moment in history? What is my reason for being *here* at *this time*?"

Engaging in a conversation with our Creator can take place by way of what many would call *prayer*. But some people are afraid of prayer, because it suggests excessive religiosity and an impersonal, almost formulaic methodology. I don't think this has to be the case. Certainly, the Scriptures teach some principles for effective prayer, chief among them that God honors the humble, honest, sincere heart. Effective prayer subordinates one's personal desires to the will of God. Effective prayer does not only seek one's own well-being, but also seeks the well-being of others. It goes beyond simply acknowledging that God exists, to believing that God is active, present, and loving enough to hear your prayer and answer your prayer in God's own way and in God's own time.

I do believe, however, that you cannot be so heavenly minded that you are of no earthly good. I recognize that the fullest expression of my relationship with God is not only in my private times of prayer and worship. How I express my relationship with God is just as important in the public square as it is in my private prayer. I believe that one's relationship with God should be both personal and public. While many people think that one's faith should be strictly a personal and private matter, I do not subscribe to that philosophy.

Make no mistake about it: one's relationship with God should be—and must be—intensely personal. It is individual.

It is as idiosyncratic to you as is your DNA. But it is not intended to be private. It is not solely meant to be expressed in empty platitudes and "I LOVE JESUS" bumper stickers, and T-shirts with witty religious sayings—although they can be effective in their own way—but it is meant to be expressed in how you love other people. It is to be expressed in what you do with your day. It is to be expressed in how you steward your resources. It is to be expressed in how you bounce back from failure. It is to be expressed in how you celebrate and attribute your victories.

The apostle James, the half brother of Jesus, wrote that faith without works is dead. It is not that works define faith, but rather that true faith motivates good works. Some of faith is expressed in silence, rest, and deep self-reflection, when we are still enough to hear the quiet whisper of God's voice leading us. But true faith finds its fullest expression in the behaviors that manifest outwardly from one's own heart and soul. Faith is expressed in both miraculous and mundane moments. Faith is expressed in the stubborn refusal to let the difficulty of your present circumstances cause you to abandon the calling you have received from God.

An old hymn written by Methodist preacher Charles Tindley talks about how we will understand things better by and by. You don't get all of the details of why you were made and how you will express your life's work upfront on day one. A prayer to gain greater clarity or understanding about your purpose is not going to give you a detailed forecast of the next seventy-five years. In my experience, God will give you enough to be faithful right now, because in some cases, if we saw the entire script, we would run away and abort God's plan.

So you receive enough of an assignment in front of you to be faithful today. Which is why I go back to the ultimate purpose, which is to glorify God. If I can glorify God in being faithful to what God has put in front of me today, and if I steward the time and steward the energy and steward my resources in a way that honors what God has given me to do in this particular moment, then I will be all right. What comes next is in many ways predicated upon your faithfulness to this point and your obedience to the direction you have received so far.

For the young people who are on the front end of life trying to figure this out—especially teenagers and twenty-somethings at some important inflection points that will determine the trajectory of their lives—if this is you, you have the opportunity to make decisions in an intentional way. This is the concept of surrendering your life to Christ. It is not merely about a religious conversion experience. It is literally saying, "God, I derive my purpose from my identity in you, so take my life, because its purpose is whatever you want it to be. Take it. Mold it. Have it. Do with it what you will."

This is not to be mistaken for a misguided passivity that assumes that the omnipotent God will work everything out without human effort. On the contrary, acknowledging the hand of God in your life motivates you to do your best. In the words of Saint Benedict, it makes you pray as though everything depends on God and then work as if everything depends on you. The notion of surrendering one's life to the control and to the pleasure of the God of the universe is about partnering with God every day of your life. And the earlier you start, the longer the runway for God to do amazing things in your life and through your life.

This equally applies to the person who is in their forties, fifties, sixties, seventies, or even eighties or nineties; I know many who come to faith in the latter years of their lives. As the saying goes, "It's not the years in your life, it's the life in your years." It is never too late to discover your reason for being and devote as much life and strength as you have left to live into your purpose every day.

4

Am I Running the Right Race?

To be nobody-but-yourself—in a world which is doing its best ... to make you everybody else—means to fight the hardest battle which any human being can fight ...

—E. E. CUMMINGS

As we get older (or *better,* as some of us would say), moving from young adulthood to middle age, many of us eventually encounter something called the *midlife crisis.* This is when we reach the point in our lives, generally when we're in our forties or fifties, that we begin to question whether we are running the right race—whether we're on the right path to achieve our purpose and ultimately leave behind the legacy we envision. While humans have likely suffered midlife crises for centuries, it wasn't until a Canadian psychologist, Elliott Jaques, wrote an article, "Death and the Mid-Life Crisis," published in 1965 in the *International Journal of Psycho-Analysis,* that the nomenclature for this phenomenon crystallized. In his article, Jaques wrote:

A person who reaches mid-life, either without having successfully established himself in marital or occupational life, or having established himself by means of manic activity and denial with consequent emotional impoverishment, is badly prepared for meeting the demands of middle age, and getting enjoyment out of this maturity. In such cases, the mid-life crisis, and the adult encounter with the conception of life to be lived in the setting of an approaching personal death, will likely be experienced as a period of psychological disturbance and depressive breakdown.[1]

While the power that this crisis exerts on us varies from person to person—with some making it through their midlife relatively unscathed and others plunging into the depths of despair and even clinical depression—researchers have shown that the midlife crisis is genuine. An article in *The Economist* explores something called "the U-bend of life," when feelings of happiness and well-being decline from youth to middle age, and then improve again as people get older. According to the article, "People are least happy in their 40s and early 50s. They reach a nadir at a global average of 46."[2]

What could be the source of this U-bend in happiness and well-being, and why do so many people experience it? I believe that one of the critical questions with which we must wrestle is, "Am I running the right race?" Not having a meaningful or satisfactory answer that fits with our calling could translate into unhappiness or crisis at any point in life.

When the answer to that question is yes, then life is good—that's one less thing to worry about. However, when the answer to the question is no, or "I don't really know," then deep contentment and well-being may be slightly more difficult to come by.

Before she became a world-renowned French chef, television personality, and cookbook author, Julia Child worked as an advertising manager for a furniture store and then as an assistant for William Donovan, the director of the Office of Strategic Services (OSS), during World War II, where she eventually served as an intelligence officer. The OSS was the predecessor to the Central Intelligence Agency.

Before her 1985 breakout acting role as Celie in the film version of *The Color Purple*, Whoopi Goldberg worked as a beautician and makeup artist at a funeral parlor. Since then, she has acted in over 150 films, and beginning in 2007, has served as the moderator for the popular television talk show *The View*. She is one of only a few people to win an Oscar, a Grammy, a Tony, and an Emmy.

And, before finding her niche as a daytime talk-show host, Ellen DeGeneres worked as a bartender, an oyster shucker, a paralegal, a stand-up comic, and a television sitcom actress. She has hosted her popular syndicated television show, *The Ellen DeGeneres Show*, for more than fifteen years, with an average of 2.9 million viewers per episode.

Each of these people discovered during the course of their lives that they were running the wrong race. But instead of accepting their lot as an advertising manager, a makeup artist in a funeral parlor, or an oyster shucker, they continued to strive to align their lives with their calling—their highest and best use. And through much introspection, hard work, and perseverance, each did exactly that.

Our Creator has a plan for us, and it is up to us to live it as fully as we can. Living beneath the potential of our highest and best use should be an unacceptable prospect. If we find ourselves stuck in a life that is not aligned with God's calling on our lives, then we have the power to make a change.

Indeed, we have the *responsibility* to make whatever changes are necessary to get ourselves in position to faithfully engage our life's work.

What Race Are We Running?

Each of us has a set of routines that characterizes our daily lives. For many of us, the script goes something like this: we wake up, jump in the shower, grab some breakfast, take the kids to school, make the commute to work, and spend the majority of our waking hours on the job. And then we reverse the sequence at the end of the workday, eventually landing back in bed and fast asleep until the next morning, when the daily routine starts all over again.

For the most part, we don't think much about these routines: we are on autopilot as we work our way through them. They are so much a part of us that we don't step back to consider why we do them or whether we even should at all. We just perform them, day in and day out.

But sometimes—maybe in the stillness of the early morning, or in a quiet moment of contemplation—we may stop to consider if our daily routines are the right ones, if we are running the right race. When I think about running the right race, three words come to mind in terms of how a number of people might occupy themselves each day: "job," "career," and "vocation." These three words are often used interchangeably, but I believe they are distinct.

Etymologists speculate that the idea of a *job* first came about in the mid-seventeenth century to refer to a piece of work or a task that's completed in exchange for compensation. The word "career" derives from the Latin, referring to a cart or wheeled vehicle, and it comes to us through the French language to denote a road or racetrack, suggesting that one's career is defined as going around in circles. No wonder so many of us feel that we are making precious little progress—if any at all—in our careers!

"Vocation," on the other hand, derives from the Latin word for "calling." It's something one receives and for which one listens. American theologian and writer Frederick

Buechner describes "vocation" as "the place where your deep gladness and the world's deep hunger meet."[3] Educator and activist Parker Palmer describes "vocation" as "something I can't not do."[4] According to Palmer, he sees vocation "not as a goal to be achieved but as a gift to be received."[5]

To me, vocation is not just doing what you most enjoy, or pursuing your passion or what makes you happy. In fact, I believe a calling does not have anything to do with the pursuit of happiness at all, though living out one's calling may bring enjoyment and fulfillment. It does not even necessarily reflect the most common use of one's skills and talents, though skills and talents may prove useful in one's vocation. It is all about being on your purpose path.

There are several ancient stories of individuals who did not feel especially well suited or particularly inclined to carry out the work of their vocations. Moses' story in the Scriptures comes to mind, about being called to lead the children of Israel out of slavery. He resisted that call. He had shortcomings and insecurities that made him feel ill-suited for that call, but he lived it out nonetheless, with the help of God.

Jeremiah was called to be a prophet. God said, "Before you were born, I knew you and I called you to this work." Jeremiah resisted that call. He said, "I'm young, I have limitations, I don't feel particularly well suited for this." Even later in his ministry, he thought about stopping because of some obstacles that he faced. But then he recognized that the message he was called to spread was like fire shut up in his bones—he couldn't *not* do what he was called to do.

Jesus' purpose was the salvation of the world and the redemption and reconciliation of humankind back to God. Dying on the cross was not glamorous. In fact, Jesus asked the Father if there was any way possible to not have to embrace that part of the assignment. Knowing that the answer was no, Jesus did it anyway. Vocation is not about passion, enjoyment, or excitement. It's about doing what you were put on this earth to do—to do what you can't *not* do. And even though there is no immediate glamor or warm-and-fuzzy feeling that comes with living into one's calling, there is a deep joy that beckons us into an ever more courageous and complete obedience to the call.

The journey may be grueling, inconvenient, uncomfortable, and even undesirable, but the fulfillment of knowing you are doing what you have been called to do is worth it. *That's* running the right race.

In cases like some of the stories I just described, we are often tempted to look at certain remarkable lives and point to pinnacles of achievement and assume that there was a degree of inevitability to them. Hindsight is always twenty-twenty, but making the commitment to live out one's calling—one courageous decision at a time—is not easy, and "success" as others define it is not certain.

The Calling That Matters Most

There must be a caller if there is going to be a calling. I believe that there are many voices attempting to construct callings for us. Sometimes it is our own voice, sometimes it is the voice of society, sometimes it is the voice of the family, sometimes it is the voice of a boss or someone else who has ambition for you. But ultimately, if God is both the Creator and Caller—and I believe God is—then it's God's calling that matters most.

For those people who may struggle with their belief in God and view God as an impersonal force, I would propose an alternate view. God is not a distant, impersonal deity who calls us and leaves us to fend for ourselves, but rather a very personal, very present, very concerned, and very invested Father whose will is to facilitate the fullest expression of His call in our lives—for His pleasure and glory, but also for our greater good.

God not only has a plan for each individual, but God also has a plan for *all* of creation down through the ages. There is no event in human history that has taken God by surprise. There is no event in any individual's life that has caught God off guard. There's no event that's taking place in my life or yours that has caught God asleep at the wheel. God is sovereign and always in control.

There are some things that God orchestrates, there are some things that God allows, but in the words of the apostle Paul's letter to the early church at Rome, the promise we have is that in all these things, God is at work for our ultimate benefit if we love Him and are called according to *His* purpose.

His purpose for us, then, with a deeper examination of that text from Romans 8:28, is not financial gain, nor personal comfort, nor even personal satisfaction. God is always at work to form and refine the real you—the deeper self beyond the flesh and bones to make us look more and more like the character of Jesus Christ. The closer we get to Jesus' character, the closer we are to becoming our highest and best selves.

The Benefits of Running the Right Race

To understand the benefits of running the right race, we must first realize that it's not all about the benefits. There may be pain, there may be discomfort, there may be inconvenience and even suffering when we choose to run the right race.

Not everyone has the same opportunity to decide what they want to be when they grow up and what to do with their lives with respect to their daily work. Many people across the globe must seek whatever employment opportunities may be found so they can put food on their family's table and clothes on their children's backs.

My own great-grandfather was a wage worker who dyed fabrics in a cotton mill. In terms of his formal training, he only had the benefit of a second-grade elementary-school education, but he did what he had to do to care for his family. There is no shame in having to put in an honest day's work for an honest day's pay. But many of us *do* have the ability to choose which work we'd like to do. This is where the importance of aligning our daily work with our life's work comes into sharper focus.

The question "What's in it for me?" is often applied to the concept of choosing a career. Many people assume that by getting on a desirable career path, they will aquire what they want in life; however, they get on the wrong track and find themselves trapped and dissatisfied. Many people think of money, prestige, and status as the key rewards to seek, but increasingly, workers are far more attracted to opportunities for personal and professional growth, opportunities for creativity and innovation, and opportunities to be a part of a team committed to advancing a meaningful purpose beyond maximizing shareholder value. These are important and worthy aims that individuals cannot necessarily expect their companies to provide for them; they must often be sought after.

There was a time when companies were like families. You could depend on a certain implicit social contract between yourself and your employer—that if you did right by the company, the company would do right by you. As long as you did the right things, the company would invest in you and your family and care about your career growth and well-being. Upon your retirement, they'd host a celebration in your honor, perhaps award you with a gold watch or keepsake clock, and fund a pension that lasted until your death. Those days are just about over in most companies around the world.

Nowadays, most people are not able to depend on their companies for such family-like care—and many are not even able to count on their companies to be fair and do what's right, not to mention help navigate career progress. Instead, people are being treated like commodities that can be acquired and released at the company's pleasure and whim. Now you're responsible for finding your own way and charting your own course within an organization— and perhaps now more than ever, *between* organizations. You're responsible for advocating for and pursuing your own development and well-being.

That's why for many people—especially millennials— the question "What's in it for me?" points directly to the pursuit of impact and purpose. This *purpose* motive—to feel like one's time, energy, and talent is going toward the advancement of a greater, meaningful end—is guiding the career decisions of many highly skilled workers. And unfortunately, it is a need that many companies are not built to meet.

We see this purpose motive animating professional behavior like never before. We see highly skilled people who are willing to volunteer their time and talents after working very long hours in demanding careers, all in the name of contributing to a greater purpose. They are willing to give you more of their time after work at no cost as volunteers for the causes they believe in because of the purpose motive.

Wikipedia's website is maintained through the purpose motive, as countless volunteers from all over the world contribute the content that many of us take for granted. You can think of the open-source software ecosystem, including such software platforms as Apache or Linux, as existing—and thriving—because of the purpose motive. People who could be out making use of their skill sets for lots and lots of money are instead willing to give of their effort freely and generously based on the purpose motive. Even at many of the world's top business schools, we're seeing a trend of more students eschewing some of the traditionally prestigious career paths, instead opting for opportunities to create social impact. This speaks volumes.

This is not about pursuing happiness, however. Purpose and happiness are not the same. For individuals, I believe that happiness can result from living out one's purpose, but it is not the end itself. I would look at it more as a matter of joy. Happiness is about what's happening and how I feel about it. Joy is a far less transient and circumstantial state of being. There's a permanence and a transcendence in joy that supersedes the day-to-day roller-coaster-like ride of one's happiness. There is deep joy that can be found in one's work, though walking in one's calling is not a fun day every day.

When living a life that is vocationally courageous—

when you have received and are walking in your calling—there will be difficulties, there will be bumps, there will be bruises, there will be dark seasons. There are difficult conversations to be had. There are difficult times to be endured. But through it all you will be sustained in knowing that you are spending your life doing something that is not only worthwhile to someone else but worthwhile to God.

How Do You Know You're Running the Right Race?

When people question whether they are running the right race, they have traditionally asked, "What am I called to do?" This is the fifty-thousand-foot level, which can honestly be rather daunting. Instead, it may be easier to first consider more pragmatic questions: "What am I doing every day? Is it aligned with my values? And, not only with my values, but is my daily work aligning with my life's work?" Running the right race is a matter of our life's work, and the activities we choose to engage in each day define whether we run the race well. What we have done with our days determines what we have done with our life.

There are libraries full of good books on career navigation. There are libraries full of books on following your passion, avoiding career pitfalls, and career burnout. This is not one of those books. This book is about listening for one's calling in life, connecting to the Caller, and expressing that life's work to the fullest extent possible through one's daily work.

A calling is not pursuing the pathway of self-interest or selfish ambition. It's the essence of who you are created to be and the alignment that you can experience between your daily work and your life's work. There's a *glow* within us when we have a deep knowing that we are where we belong. There's an almost metaphysical element to it, when you look at yourself and see that you are in the exact place where you belong right now. You know you're in the right place. You know it in your soul and you can feel it in your bones. This is the work that you cannot *not* do with your life.

I want to emphasize the need for each of us not only to be deeply self-reflective but to develop a spiritual relationship with God for ourselves. There's no substitute for that. The five questions that organize this book have helped me in coaching others and clarifying their unique life's work and in advising how to navigate through the twists and turns to align their life's work with their daily work. But there's no substitute for hearing God for yourself.

This path is unique for every one of us. Not only is each person's God-given calling unique, but so is each person's path to discovering it. I knew I was called to Christian ministry at age seven, but that did not begin finding its expression in the life of a congregation until over a decade later. And I did not become a pastor until I was twenty-six.

I had no idea that being a professor in a business school would be a core part of my calling until I was in my mid-twenties. Yes, everyone has a purpose path, but it's rarely straightforward—there are twists, turns, forks in the road, and unpaved ground. Sometimes, we are called to carve out paths that do not yet exist so that someone coming behind us can find *their* way.

While this book can highlight for you the value of listening for your calling and perhaps even provide guidance around how you might go about it, this book cannot replace the voice of God in your life. It's impossible. Any book that would promise to do so, other than the Scriptures, is overpromising and guaranteed to woefully underdeliver. You have to listen for the voice of your Caller so that you can find *your* way.

The Danger of Running Someone Else's Race

The blessing of having role models living out their calling is that you see it can be done. But at the same time, the danger of seeing role models living out their calling is that you want to emulate what they're doing instead of emulating their relentless commitment to their calling. The danger lies in wanting to run someone else's race.

When people want to run someone else's race, it is usually because they find something worthy of emulation and imitation in the other person. Perhaps it is because we see what the person has accomplished and amassed. Or perhaps we see the person's reputation and the recognition that they receive for living out their calling.

In reality, we often see them on their best days and in the best possible way. It's not wrong to have role models. It's not wrong to have mentors and coaches. In fact, I would encourage everybody to have both—and perhaps multiples of each in their lives. However, imitating or mimicking what someone does is not going to get you what someone else has. You may be able to imitate their *what*, but you cannot imitate their *why*.

PROFILE IN COURAGE: *Juan Diaz*

One of my former students, Juan Diaz, represents the third generation of his family to work in the family business, a food-service supply distributor based in Venezuela. He spent his entire childhood in and around the business, and the fact that he'd perhaps succeed his father as CEO someday seemed all but inevitable. Before business school, he worked as an account manager. He came to me for coaching because he didn't want to disappoint his father by telling him that he wanted to leave the family business to explore other opportunities. He wasn't sure what he wanted to do with his life, but after our first coffee chat, he knew for sure what he *didn't* want to do—stay with the family business. His parents were none too pleased to learn of Juan's desire to leave, especially since he didn't know what he wanted to do. He wanted to use his analytical skill to make a difference in the world, but he didn't exactly know how.

He entered the world of management consulting as a temporary professional detour to provide him some additional exposure and hone his business acumen to position him for his next move. Like Juan, sometimes knowing what you *don't* feel called to do is a meaningful and necessary step toward what you *are* called to do with your life.

You may recall the story in chapter 3 of the three men who were laying bricks to build a cathedral. Each of the three men had very different perceptions and conceptions of what it was they were doing and why it mattered. Let's imagine for a moment that I decide to stop what I'm doing and start laying bricks alongside them—hoping to find my own *why*. That would be well and good, but I'm going to miss some fundamental things.

I'm not going to have the same sense of *why* that they have. If I'm simply mimicking their activity and their actions, that won't lead me to better understand my unique why and what I should be doing about it. You'll never be able to mimic someone else's why because it's *his or her* why. You have to figure out your own for yourself. The sorts of questions that authors such as Frederick Buechner, Parker Palmer, and others have posed over the years are illuminating, and they have the power to spark deep insights.

What is it that brings you deep joy and fulfillment? What problems do you really want to solve? What would you do if you never got paid another day, but you would do it for the rest of your life? What would that be? These are great questions, but at the end of the day, trying to run someone else's race results in the catastrophe of you not being the best and highest self you were designed to become.

It's cute when little kids mimic and parrot their parents. While it's cute when you're a kid, it could be catastrophic if you're an adult just mimicking and parroting other adults without clarity around why they're doing what they're doing. I think the danger of trying to run someone else's race is that you could be doing harm to yourself and harm to those around you. You don't need to be a mindless clone of someone else; be the best *you* that you can be. There is a race for everyone, and no two paths are the same.

Discovering vocation doesn't mean scrambling toward some prize just beyond your reach, but rather accepting the treasure that you have been given. But make no mistake about it, well-meaning people around you—friends, family, work associates, and others—will push you to run someone else's race. Perhaps their own. As E. E. Cummings once said:

To be nobody-but-yourself—in a world which is doing its best, night and day, to make you everybody else—means to fight the hardest battle which any human being can fight; and never stop fighting.[6]

Understanding who you are and not trying to become someone else is challenging, and our current environment can make it even more difficult. For as long as there has been a news media, it has been obsessed with celebrities, whether film stars, popular musicians, athletes, politicians, powerful and wealthy people, or others that attract the attention and adulation of the public. And now social media takes this to another level altogether, creating people who have larger-than-life personas who are put forward as being worthy of worship and adoration and imitation. Some people even create fake personas that they want you to believe are the real them. That puts us on a very, very slippery slope.

Mentors, parents, teachers, caring friends, and others who love you and are concerned about you can serve as guardrails. But, sometimes—even with the best of intentions— their advice can lead you away from your unique calling. You have to process their advice through the filter of your own sense of self and your own sense of purpose.

I had many mentors tell me to either pursue the path of pastoral ministry or to pursue the path of developing expertise as a management scholar, but not both. And while they were giving me the best advice they could, many of them were giving me advice from the perspective of their *own* calling, their own path and experiences. Some even advised me based on what they'd seen others do.

But what I wrestled with most was the fact that I knew I had a unique call—a unique God-given assignment in this moment in time. I had to chew the meat and spit out the bones and be very, very prayerful. I couldn't let any other voice in my heart be louder than God's voice. That takes a lot of discipline. It's a lot easier to hear and be persuaded by human voices, because you live and work with them, because they are more easily discernible, and because they can often be quite loud and compelling.

The voice of God must beat out every other voice in your head. That is the essence of running the right race. Some of the voices of others can help you clarify how to run it well, but those voices cannot define your race for you.

Clarity and Courage

The idea of running the right race is a matter of having *clarity*, specifically, clarity of who your Caller is and what the message is on the other end of the line. Our lives are filled with well-meaning people who try to get us to run the race they think is ours. There are parents who try to get their kids to become what they could not become—without regard to what these children are uniquely well suited or positioned to do. There are spouses and significant others who push their loved ones into more lucrative, but less vocationally consistent careers. There are bosses who discourage certain employees from their preferred career tracks and pigeonhole them into something that does not resonate with them at all, just for the sake of keeping them around.

In each of these cases, parents and spouses and friends and family members or bosses or mentors are trying to get someone to run a race that they believe would be best for this person to run. And they are wrong.

So what can you do to resist the push from these well-meaning people in your life? The test is to answer this question: When you hear these other voices, how do they hit your spirit? Do they resonate in your own heart and soul with the same frequency and power as God's voice? If so, you're in great shape. If not, you've got to do the work of first identifying what the source of the dissonance is, then determining what parts of the advice might actually be worth applying at this moment.

This, of course, takes no small amount of courage. You need courage to demonstrate a commitment to living out your *why*. Vocational courage ultimately comes down to two things: clarity plus commitment—clarity around what your life's work is, and then a commitment to making whatever decisions are necessary to live it out faithfully.

This means doing your best to align your daily work and your life's work, no matter the cost. This may require you to walk away from a job or career track that you know is not consistent with your life's work, or to have a difficult conversation with a mentor, boss, spouse, friend, or parent who is trying to mold you and shape you in a way that is inconsistent with the clarity you have gained about your unique reason for being.

This is especially important for twentysomethings who may confuse *calling* with *ambition* or *aspiration*. This is *not* about self-interested or selfish ambition. This is about what your life's work is, what the net impact of your life will have been—whether it is on society at large or on the people with whom you have the privilege of interacting on a daily basis—and the people who will be impacted through your daily work.

It's important not to simply discard the advice of these well-meaning voices just for the sake of saying, "I'm going to be my own man or my own woman." But it is important to be able to distill the value that can be derived from their goodwill while not allowing what you are hearing from your Caller to become subject to what these other voices are saying.

Their voices should be subject to what God is saying to you, not God's voice subject to the affirmation of what others are saying. This is another place where courage comes into play. It's not easy to do—especially when you're young, when you are impressionable, and when you are relying on these lifelines for financial, social, and other types of support.

Consider the example of Sabrina Kay, a very successful entrepreneur in Los Angeles. Sabrina was born in South Korea, and her mother realized when Sabrina was four years old that she could pick out songs on the piano by ear—without reading music. That was all it took for Sabrina's mother to decide on the future path her daughter would take: an accomplished pianist. Says Sabrina about her mother:

> *She immediately made me take vigorous piano lessons, because that was one of the possible very successful career choices for women in South Korea . . . The piano teacher my mom found lived with us. Every time I turned around or had a moment to breathe, there he was, standing by.*[7]

However, being forced to practice piano constantly did not increase Sabrina's love for the instrument—indeed, it had quite the opposite effect. Finally, when she became a teenager and started experimenting with youthful rebellion, her primary target was the piano—and her parents' hopes and dreams for their daughter. According to Sabrina:

> *I never loved playing the piano, and being forced into lessons made me associate the piano with punishment. When I became a teenager, the first most rebellious thing I did was not sex, drugs or rock 'n' roll. I said "no" to piano. My mother was shocked. And I never played the piano again.*[8]

This moment of clarity, combined with the commitment to listen for her true calling, led Sabrina from a very difficult situation with her parents, to what she was really meant to do with her life: create a business that would help others become who *they* wanted to be.

Sabrina moved with her family to the United States when she was nineteen years old. She didn't speak a word of English when she arrived in the United States, but she quickly gained her footing—taking an incredibly intense course load each semester in college and working three jobs while pregnant with her daughter, Lina. She became a fashion designer, then started her own business: California Design College, a business that she eventually sold for millions of dollars. Today she holds a doctoral degree from the University of Pennsylvania's Wharton School and is a globally celebrated educator, entrepreneur, and philanthropist.

Of course, parents still have a profound influence on us later in life, even long after we have left their nest. We all know the stories of "helicopter" parents, who are hyper-involved with their children in elementary school. This involvement has now spread to college and even businesses, with orientations for parents being added to the regular new-student or new-employee orientations. As this heavy imprinting role of parents creeps into their children's twenties, thirties, and even forties and beyond, the more that courage will be required to live out one's unique life's work.

For many cultures, the expectation of immediate and complete deference to one's parents—no matter one's age—

is an unshakably powerful force. In some cultures, many parents believe that they have the right to select (read: *manipulate*) their young adult children's futures. In this situation, such as the strong Confucian culture in which Sabrina Kay grew up, it requires that much more courage to break free of the expectations that others have for you. And it takes action—asserting that while your parents are your earthly creators, you have a heavenly Creator who is calling you to live the life for which you were created. Remember: when someday your parents are gone, you will still be left to wrestle with your Maker.

In a speech to the 102nd NAACP National Convention, then chairman Roslyn Brock recounted a line from the film *The Help,* in which a key character reflects on her own life, telling her crusading daughter, "They say that courage sometimes skips a generation." To this, Roslyn Brock proclaimed:

> *If courage is the fuel that enables us to find inner strength, bravery and fortitude required to confront danger, difficulty, hardship and opposition . . . we must ensure that courage does not skip this generation!*[9]

Indeed, we must ensure that vocational courage does not skip a generation—or any one of us.

As we see from Sabrina Kay's story, there is a deep

dissatisfaction that results when you are not running your race. There comes a point where it's not just a matter of disillusionment or discomfort, but an abiding dissatisfaction with yourself and how you are occupying your time. You can have as much money, as much recognition, and as many credits to your name as you can imagine, but still not be fulfilled. You can have it all, but not be able to look at yourself in the mirror proudly because you know that you're not doing with your life what you're supposed to be doing with it. You're out of place, and every day is a mismatch between what you do and who you are.

Knowing who you are, and what your *why* is, ensures that you know what race it is you should be running. Vocation transcends career. It is a race against yourself. It's a race of one. Somebody may be smarter, more capable, or more effective. But the race of life is not about running faster than someone else; Scripture says that the race is not given to the swift nor the battle to the strong. The writer of the Letter to the Hebrews tells his readers to run their race with patient endurance. This is about patience, it's about clarity, it's about commitment.

There might not only be internal resistance, but external resistance as well. You might find people who will make it their mission to stand in your way and undermine your progress. You might discover people who will make it their business to attempt to thwart the fulfillment of your vocation. You may need to develop skills, be trained or further educated to fulfill your vocation. In fact, I would argue that sometimes the presence of unexpected road-blocks to navigate around and unexpected mountains to climb can often indicate that you're in the right place. Sometimes hardship is the evidence that you're in the right place. That is not to suggest that all hardship is the result of living a vocationally courageous life, but sometimes hardship can be an indicator that you are on the right path toward that life.

Recognize that God is the Caller. God is the course designer, God is your sustainer along the course. God is the reason you're on the course in the first place. When you decide your calling is yours alone to make, independent of God, you risk mistaking your ambition, your dream, or your passion for your calling. When people call themselves, they mislead themselves. The essence of having a calling is that you have *been* called.

The activities you undertake in the course of living your calling gain meaning and value in that God equips, ordains, and sustains you to carry out that work. There are a lot of people who do great work but don't have an impact. They're well-meaning, they're well educated, but they don't have impact. Or perhaps they have impact, but the impact they are making does not have deep meaning in their lives.

What separates two people with the same degree and the same skills when one makes an impact and the other doesn't? It's not all about socioeconomics, although that can sometimes be a factor. It is not all about pedigree, though that too can be a factor. It's not all about skills and social connections to influential people, though skills and connections can be helpful. It is God behind the scenes, working out a narrative in our life, the implications of which transcend time and space. God is the One who makes the difference.

While it may be difficult for us to perceive because we are fixed creatures living in time and space, it is by trusting and being able to interpret that we see in retrospect how God has taken seemingly disparate pieces and made a masterpiece. We are God's workmanship created in Christ for good works, according to Ephesians 2:10. The idea of us being God's workmanship is *poema*, the Greek word from which we get the English word "poem."

If we are God's poem, if we are God's masterpiece, there are some moments when, in the making of a masterpiece, it doesn't look very masterful. In the process of molding a piece of pottery, the potter has the clay on the wheel, but it does not look like what it's going to become. But the finished product—a beautiful, sparkling vase—is in the potter's mind from the beginning. There is intentionality.

In our lives, pressure is placed on us from a variety of different directions—sometimes to the point of breaking. But, ultimately, there is blessing if we can endure the process and not try to wiggle our way off the wheel of the potter. The blessing is in receiving and exploring our vocation and then being able to live it out to its fullest extent.

That is *true* success.

5

Am I Running the Race Well?

Do you not know that those who run in a race all run, but one receives the prize? Run in such a way that you may obtain it.

—1 CORINTHIANS 9:24

While each of us wants to work in a job that is important and makes a difference in the world around us, some jobs by their very nature require those who have them to put their own lives on the line to help others. Police, firefighters, and members of the military services come to mind, along with other hazardous jobs in the aviation, farming, fishing, logging, and roofing industries, which, according to the Bureau of Labor Statistics, suffer the most on-job fatalities. When your job requires you to put your own life at risk, then it's critically important that you are running the race well; anything less can have disastrous consequences, both for yourself and for those you are tasked to help.

The Navy SEALs—short for SEa, Air, and Land teams—

are an elite special-operations force whose members are specifically trained to take on the most hazardous military assignments. According to the Navy SEALs website, these assignments, among others, include:

- Capturing high-value enemy personnel and terrorists around the world
- Collecting information and intelligence through special reconnaissance missions
- Carrying out small-unit, direct-action missions against military targets[1]

Running the race well can quite literally make the difference between life and death for Navy SEALs and the other members of their team.

Admiral William McRaven is a former Navy SEAL who was commander of US Special Operations Command from 2011 to 2014 and served until 2018 as chancellor of the University of Texas System. Admiral McRaven knows what it means to run the race well, and he spoke about this topic when he gave the commencement address to the University of Texas at Austin Class of 2014. As McRaven explained, because of the life-and-death nature of the job, becoming a Navy SEAL is no easy task. He talked about the harsh extremes to which the trainees' bodies and minds are pushed for six months on the journey to becoming professional warriors.

However, for a young Navy recruit who hopes to

become a SEAL, this remarkably arduous training begins with a simple but critical task that has to be performed to perfection: the mundane task of *perfectly* making a bed. According to McRaven:

> *It seemed a little ridiculous at the time, particularly in light of the fact that [we] were aspiring to be real warriors, tough battle-hardened SEALs, but the wisdom of this simple act has been proven to me many times over.*
>
> *If you make your bed every morning you will have accomplished the first task of the day. . . . By the end of the day, that one task completed will have turned into many tasks completed. Making your bed will also reinforce the fact that little things in life matter. If you can't do the little things right, you will never do the big things right. . . .*
>
> *If you want to change the world, start off by making your bed.*[2]

In recent years, the University of Texas at Austin has employed the tagline, "What starts here changes the world." Admiral McRaven suggested that if each of the eight thousand members of the class of 2014 changed the lives of just ten people, and those ten individuals changed the lives of ten more, and so on, in just five generations, the class of 2014 had the potential to change the lives of eight hundred million people—more than double the population of the United States.

As we perform our chosen vocations, we have the potential to change the lives of our customers, coworkers, and the communities in which we work. If we run our race well, then we maximize the impact we have on the world around us and our spirit is strengthened. If we don't run the race well, then our impact is minimized and our spirit is weakened. This makes understanding how to run the race well, and determining whether or not we are doing so, key to finding true success in life.

Running the Race Well

It's one thing to run a race—anyone can do that—but it's another thing altogether to run the race *well*. Think about an Olympian or a professional athlete. These men and women train for years—willingly dedicating many hundreds and even thousands of hours of their lives to perfecting the athletic skills and techniques they need to win, strengthening their bodies to withstand the most difficult physical challenges, and building tremendous mental toughness and resilience along the way.

When I talk about what "running the race well" means in a vocational context, I'm thinking about how closely someone adheres to their stated values as that person is running the race that is his or her life. When someone is able to accomplish this feat—to live every aspect of career and life in accordance with his or her most deeply held values—I believe that person is truly *winning* the race.

Now perhaps more than ever, people are concerned with how to integrate the increasingly complicated professional and personal aspects of life (which many call work-life balance). How much time should we devote to our jobs and work, and how much should we reserve for family and friends? How much effort should we devote to our own spiritual, mental, and physical well-being? How many times have we heard these words from our coworkers, friends, or family? "I'm doing great in my career, but it's costing me where it matters most." Or "My family is the most important thing to me, but I am married to my job and I'm rarely able to spend time with them." Or "I ended up working the entire time I was on vacation, and my spouse was not too happy about it." Too often, I suspect, and we may even be saying these words ourselves.

I don't say this to judge or point the finger at anyone in terms of whether or not they are living out their values "correctly." Three people may say that family is most important to them—but one person shows it by working two jobs to keep their family housed and fed; another shows it by leaving work early to pick up their kids from school; another person shows it by taking their earnings and caring for their aging parents. Each of them has a value of family, but they each live it out and express it differently. I'm not looking to drive conformity around how we express our values, but rather to ask along this journey, Are you sticking to your values, and are your values animating and motivating your action as you run the race?

When your values and your actions are aligned, then you are running your race with *integrity*. And, if you run your race with integrity, by definition you run it well. By integrity, I don't just mean adherence to a particular moral code. Integrity is about oneness, wholeness—that who you say you are is expressed through your behavior. It means that your actions are consistent with your values. It means that the values you say you have are the values that guide your decisions.

For example, Hyatt Hotels Corporation, the global hospitality giant, has a core value of *care*, which they say motivates them to "care for people so they can be their best."[3] Many leaders share this underlying value of care because people flourish when they are sincerely cared for. If a leader says that care is one of his or her core values, but is never available, ignores the concerns of their people, and routinely speaks rudely and dismissively to them, at a certain point, you'll wonder whether the person is really operating with a value of care.

If care or love is my animating value, I might therefore make the decision to not make products that contribute to the disintegration of families or that work toward the physiological detriment of people. I may decide to not work for a cigarette manufacturer if I know that smoking contributes to negative societal outcomes that inhibit human flourishing.

If your values don't result in corresponding action, you might want to more closely consider whether those are really your true values.

Ultimately, it's a matter of identity. You are a child of your Creator—that is your true identity. What is your Creator telling you? As we've already discussed, other voices—those of your family, friends, colleagues at work, and many others—can be loud. They can, in fact, be deafening. But through the noise and through the clutter, you've got to have clarity regarding what your values are and not compromise them.

Escalation of Commitment

In the 1970s, Barry M. Staw—professor emeritus at Berkeley's Haas School of Business—first described an idea that he called the *escalation of commitment*. In basic terms, the idea of escalation of commitment is that, once you have taken the first step, it's easier to take the second and the third.

Consider someone who is convicted of embezzling one million dollars from the company for which he works. His intent at the outset might not have been to steal one million from his employer, but he took the first small step of submitting a fraudulent reimbursement request for a hundred-dollar dinner with his wife that he claimed was a meeting with a sales prospect. And this expanded to filing fake car mileage logs over a period of several years—

worth many thousands of dollars—and then making expensive purchases on his company credit card and having the items shipped directly to his home. Each further step was reinforced and encouraged by the previous ones, until he was finally caught.

The first time you consider compromising your values, an alarm goes off in your head that says, "This is a violation." When you hear that alarm go off, you'll do one of two things. You either thank your conscience for sounding the alarm, and then you don't go there again, or, instead, you tell yourself, "That was a false alarm—this really isn't compromising my values, and this behavior is okay."

If you choose the second path, this invariably leads you to become more desensitized to the behavior the more you do it. The first time you heard that alarm in your head blaring loudly. The second time and the third time, it was not quite as loud. By the seventeenth or twentieth time, you probably will have desensitized your brain to not sound that alarm at all. The die will be cast, and you'll tend to continue to compromise your values—or even actively and routinely violate them.

When it comes to values-driven action—whether as a leader, a parent, a citizen, or a human being—it's easier to live out your values 100 percent of the time than it is to live them out even 99 percent of the time. That 1 percent can be deadly. This is why it's so important not to compromise your values—even just a little bit or even just once. Once you do it the first time—no matter how small the compromise might be—it becomes easier the second and third time you do it.

Measuring How Well You're Running the Race

From a career perspective, many career coaches lay out a series of potential rewards that people can get from their careers. They do this to see which rewards individuals value the most and which ones they value the least. These potential rewards can be anything from a particular level of income, to intellectual stimulation, recognition, autonomy, power, influence, or being able to live a certain lifestyle. These are all metrics that others use to define what it means to be successful.

When it comes to vocation, however, I look less to external metrics of success and more to people's faithfulness to what their Caller has assigned them to do. If, at the end of the day, you can look at yourself in the mirror and know that you were faithful to what you were given to do, that you did not compromise, then I believe that you have run the race well. It's not necessary that you executed 100 percent flawlessly on everything, and it's not necessary that you were perfect. I'm not perfect, and nobody else is, either. You don't have to be perfect in order to be faithful. This is not about perfection, but rather about the inclination of one's heart, head, and hands toward the fulfillment of the unique assignment you've been given to do.

If you can say that you have been a faithful steward over the resources that have been given to you in service of accomplishing your assignment, that is faithfulness, and that is success. I hasten to add that those other metrics are not inherently opposed to faithfulness. Faithfulness may or may not result in financial gain or influence or intellectual satisfaction. Those things may be positive consequences but are not necessarily indicators of one's faithfulness. You can be faithful and have little to no wealth, recognition, or power. I believe that simple, everyday faithfulness is underrated.

It's the Journey, Not Just the Destination

Vocation is all about discovery—it's a journey, an exploration of self. You might have clarity about what you need to know today, but tomorrow's a new day, with its own set of challenges and opportunities. Of course, you're not starting entirely from scratch each day; much of the knowledge and processes you have already put into place will carry over. But you will constantly encounter transition zones, pivot points where you are shifting from one platform to another as a new expression of your vocation. Today you may be trying frantically to arrange a fifty-piece puzzle, but then tomorrow you get twelve more pieces. Your goal is to be in a place each day where you can receive fresh revelations and be faithful about connecting the dots of what's in your heart, the opportunities that are before you, and which way to go. Faithfulness is measured one decision at a time.

Many of us have become more preoccupied with what we'd like to be than who we are becoming. Many of us emphasize the destination more than the journey, and the product more than the process. But vocation is not about a destination or an end goal; it is all about the process of listening, receiving, and becoming.

I believe that many of us harbor a preoccupation with being busy. Needing to always be busy doing something often steals our attention away from the still moments of life in which we experience the gift of receiving vocational direction. The ceaseless striving of overprogrammed, overscheduled lives robs us of the patience that's required to discover vocation.

I'm not saying that everyone needs to take a silent retreat every ninety days in order to figure this out, although many people will find that to be very helpful. I have found silent retreats to be a wonderful balm for the stressed, weary, restless soul. Nevertheless, the fact remains that the need to be busy—to do, do, do, produce, produce, produce— often flies in the face of running the race well, because vocation is about who you are *becoming* as much as it is about what you are *doing*.

We are always in a state of becoming our best selves, not just doing our best deeds. I love the slogan that the

Northwestern University health-care system adopted as a motto for some time: "Best is an endpoint. Better is a quest." Our lives and our vocations should be much more a quest and much less an endpoint. The quest is making our best better than it was before.

It's not about me trying to be better than someone else's best, because their best has nothing to do with me being faithful and becoming my best and bettering that. This is about growth, this is about maturation. This is about *becoming*, not just *doing*. Our society is very clear about doing, with questions like "What have you done for me lately?" Or "Are you being productive?" Or "Are you wasting time?"

But relatively few people are actually concerned about your formation as an individual—your development as a person. Development is not just about the life of the mind and intellectual stimulation—it is about the real you who will outlast your body. Who are *you* becoming? Who have you been called to become?

The Impact of Your Values on Running the Race Well

Your values define the lines that you will not cross in running your race. Your values define the race itself but also provide guidance to you around which lines you won't cross.

There's an exercise I do with some of my students that illustrates this point well. I ask them to write down, on three separate pieces of paper, their top-three most-important values in life. Once everyone has written down their top-three values, I tell them to take a look at the piece of paper that lists their number-one most-important value and to share their number-one value with those around them. After they experience a strong sense of pride in articulating their single-most important value, I tell them to pick up the piece of paper that lists that number-one value and to crumple it into a ball and throw it on the floor. I ask them to reflect on what would happen in their lives if that value was missing. How much worse and less meaningful would their lives be without this most-important value?

After everyone has crumpled up their number-one value, I ask the group, "What are you left with?" They're left with two values that are very important to them. I ask the participants to hold up these values and discuss them with their colleagues for a few minutes. How does it feel? Then I say, "Crumple up your second most-important value and throw it away."

Invariably, many of the participants will start to react. Besides the skeptical participant who says, "It's just a piece of paper for me; my values are in my heart," many will have visceral reactions: they actually start to feel sick to their stomach because they recognize that they are crumpling up their values and throwing them away. They're espousing one set of values but exemplifying another. The shame and urgency that comes across many of their faces is profound.

The point I make through this exercise is the apparent mismatch between what they *say* is valuable and what they *show* is valuable. They do this in their daily lives through decisions that are not aligned, through how they spend their time, through how they spend their energy, and through how they distribute their resources, whatever those resources may be. The exercise gets people to think as they pursue their dreams and goals: Are they violating their values in the process? Or perhaps even more important, is the goal they are pursuing a violation of their values itself? Is the fact that they're even doing this with their time a violation? Is there any way for them, knowing who they are, knowing why they're here on this earth, and knowing what their values are, to be spending their days doing what they're doing? This is where the values piece comes in—the questioning of what they should be doing in the first place.

Courage comes in once you have clarity regarding what you need to be doing. You cannot be held accountable for doing what you do not know to do. However, once you have heard the voice of your Caller, you are accountable for being faithful. How do you now orient yourself to doing that amid the many voices and the practical inconveniences of having to switch course? Saying no to people, saying no to opportunities. How do I go about doing that? That's a question I answer in the next section of this book.

Integrity and Vocational Courage

Vocational courage is about aligning one's daily work with one's life's work. *Integrity* is about being your true, authentic self and expressing that consistently, each and every day. Vocation is part and parcel of who you are. Just as function determines form, and just as strategy determines structure, our life's work should determine our daily activities. If, in fact, you have clarity around who you are and who you are called to become, then how faithfully you express that in your daily work and in your daily activities is a matter of vocational courage.

This requires stepping back to assess your daily work and taking an honest look at it. And it requires asking not just, "Am I satisfied, and do I feel fulfilled?" or even, "Is this creating some kind of social good?"; it requires digging deep and asking, "Is this what I'm called to do? Is this who I am? Does this advance the work of God in the way that God has called me to advance it? And does this mold me into the person God would have me to be?" If not, then what you are doing with your life is not vocationally courageous, even if it is having a positive impact on others.

I fully understand and respect that there are people who don't have the luxury of aligning their daily work with this concept of *vocation*. But even many such individuals will tell you that they have a profound sense of purpose that provides deep meaning to their work, often in service of others. Vocational courage has absolutely nothing to do with the glamor or the prestige of one's professional role. It is about whether you are in the right place at the right time to make the impact you are uniquely designed to make.

This brings us to a fundamental question: Does impact excuse disintegrity? That is, does the positive impact of the good works I do in my life outweigh the negative impact of acting in ways that are disingenuous?

The short answer is no—not at all.

Integrity is how you conduct yourself in the process. Impact is the by-product of the process—an outgrowth of what you did along the path. And as we have discussed, your faithfulness is the key metric of success, not the scale or scope of your impact. Making an impact does not relieve one from the responsibility of solid character. God's purpose is to make us more like Christ. God does not need any of us to do anything that God Himself could not accomplish.

God could, in a supernatural way, make anything happen on earth; God does not need human intervention or effort to create impact. God needed no human help creating the heavens and the earth. God required no human help in fashioning the human heart to beat without an apparent cause. God requires no human help in causing the sun to rise each day in the east and set in the west. God requires no human help in the rotation of the earth on its axis each day or the revolution of the earth around the sun each year. I am fully persuaded of God's ability to make things happen absent human intervention.

Nevertheless, God has mysteriously elected to engage us flawed human beings in executing the project of His will. There is no amount of impact that can excuse dishonoring God in the process. The ends do not justify the means. The means are just as important as the ends, and some might go even so far as to say that the means are themselves the ends.

Think for a moment about athletes who have accomplished great things, but once it was found that they were acting without integrity—that they cheated—the outcome didn't matter anymore. Sadly, the highest levels of sports and athletics are riddled with men and women who have asterisks next to their names. After Rosie Ruiz won the women's division of the Boston Marathon in 1980, it was discovered that she had disappeared from the course for some time, then mysteriously reappeared less than a mile from the finish line. Bicycle racer Lance Armstrong famously lied for years about his doping with performance-enhancing drugs—all while racking up win after win. As a result, an Olympic bronze medal and seven Tour de France victories were taken away from him. There are many, many other athletes who falsely believed the ends justified the means. And in every case they were wrong.

Of course, in business there are people who do the same thing. They falsely believe that growing their company or achieving certain revenue or profit goals, beating the competition, requires doing whatever it takes to win— even if they have to break the law or act unethically to do it. What's different is that, while we as sports fans tend not to excuse the bad behavior of athletes (Pete Rose—one of the greats of baseball history—has been frozen out of professional baseball and the Hall of Fame since he was accused of betting on baseball in 1989), we often excuse the bad behavior of businesspeople.

Why? I think there's a presumption on the part of many people that business is already not completely honest by its very nature. I want to push against that. You can develop market-driven solutions to intractable social dilemmas. I believe that some people are vocationally positioned to provide leadership in the marketplace as an expression of their calling and life's work. This goes back to an idea expressed by Max Weber, the philosopher and economist, an idea that actually predated him. But he captured it and wrote about it in his book *The Protestant Ethic and the Spirit of Capitalism*. Weber says that work as calling can be very important—it has a religious significance because God sets us to this vocation—and that by its inherent definition, very little work can be thought of as bad work, but the question is the motive underneath it and the impact of it.

What Can We Do If We're Not Running the Race Well?

For a variety of reasons, we may look up one day and realize that we're not running the race that is our life well. What can be done then?

I hope this book provides some relevant insights regarding what you might do next. As I've explained, you have to have the courageous conversation with your Creator about who you are, why you are, and then begin to figure out if you are truly willing to do what it takes to run the race as well as you've been designed to run it.

You are not stuck. You are not trapped. You are only as trapped as your brain lets you think you are. Every day you wake up in the morning is a new day to do something different, to make wrongs right. It's called resilience. You could be running the race poorly from an integrity perspective, but today you can commit to living with integrity for the rest of your life. Each new day is an opportunity to start afresh. Today can be a pivotal turning point—a line of demarcation between a life that others encouraged you to pursue but wasn't faithful to who you are and who you've been called to become, and a life that you can be proud of. You can experience a sense of fulfillment in life without keeping score of how many material possessions you've gained or how much recognition you've received. Being proud of your life itself is different from being proud of what you have gained in your life.

That's where the courage part comes in. It's a courageous conversation to admit and acknowledge that, within the sanctuary of your own soul, something's off. To admit to yourself, "I'm not in the right spot"—that's tough, especially if you pride yourself on being prized and recognized and applauded. You have the outward trappings of success, but you tell yourself, "I am successful but am I not a success. I am important but my life lacks significance." That's a hard conversation, and it takes no small amount of courage to have it. It also takes courage to have the conversation with those around you who are either benefiting from or are partly responsible for you being where you are.

It's not just about saying, "I'm clear on what my life's work is now. I get what vocation means." It's a process of continual reflection, exploration, and recalibration.

Beautiful. You've let your life speak. You have listened to the voice of God, and you understand what you're supposed to do. Now what?

This is the opportunity to put your proverbial money where your mouth is. To apply your time, your talent, and perhaps even your treasure to the accomplishment of your unique life's work every day. The courage part will involve some disentangling, some unbraiding. Which is why those who have just graduated from high school or college or who are in their teens, twenties, and thirties are in an ideal position to have this conversation. You don't have to do as much untangling and unbraiding as does someone who is older. You can build this vocationally courageous life from the ground up. You can start as early as when your parents ask you the age-old question "What are you going to be when you grow up?"

And if you are older, perhaps in mid-career and want to make the shift to a vocation more aligned with your life's work, or perhaps you're nearing retirement and you want to figure out what's next for you, then the time is now. Until the moment you take your last breath, you have the power within you to change your path—and your life. Again, courage is required. In the next chapter, we'll take a closer look at where this courage comes from and how we can use it to our advantage.

PART II

Putting Vocational Courage to Work

The purpose of life is to discover your gift. The work of life is to develop it. The meaning of life is to give your gift away. —DAVID VISCOTT

Once you understand what it is that you are meant to do with your life, then you have the opportunity and the responsibility to put this knowledge to work. In this part of the book, I further explore a variety of topics that will help you do just that. I begin with a deep dive into the courage side of the vocational equation, considering how to turn courage into a mind-set and habit, the best time to make a shift to align your daily work with your life's work, what to do if you can't find the courage you need when you need it, and the importance of living a faithful life to steward your vocation.

I next take a close look at how we can periodically recheck our alignment to ensure that we are still pursuing the vocation to which we have been called, or if we need a mid-course correction. I consider how best to approach a transition zone in your life, what to do if you miss your exit, and how to reach out to your lifelines (including God) for help.

Then I explore how you can help others develop vocational courage—considering the importance of being in service to others and exactly what you can do to help. I review some of the most effective approaches for coaching others to discover and hold on to vocational courage for themselves.

Finally, I consider the role of vocational courage in organizations—what vocational courage is in an organizational context, and how for-profit and nonprofit organizations can apply the principles of vocational courage to discover their own unique purpose in the world and then pursue it through their key activities and performance metrics, getting back on track if they lose their way in trying to undertake activities that do not align with their core reason for being.

6

What's Courage Got to Do with It?

You can choose courage, or you can choose comfort, but we can't have both.

—BRENÉ BROWN

Carolyn Cross served for almost six years as executive director (ED) of a local youth empowerment non-profit located outside of Boston, after a three-decade-long career with the same organization. Bucking the trend of bouncing around from organization to organization to get experience and exposure, she ascended the ranks of the organization, starting as a volunteer, then moving into a program-assistant role, eventually taking a program-manager job in 2001. After an unexpected executive departure in 2013, Carolyn accepted the offer to take the organization's helm and retained me as her coach. She quickly discovered that being the chief executive afforded a tremendous opportunity to make an impact in an organization for which she cared a great deal, but the stress of the role combined with the fact that she wasn't able to interact with the kids as much led her to retire, which let her step back from the ED role and return to her passion of working directly with kids as a volunteer in one of the organization's signature programs. Certainly stepping back from a high-powered executive role is never an easy decision, but she took a courageous step that looked like a downgrade to many in order to live the life she felt most compelled to live. She felt that she was in the right place but in the wrong role and did what was necessary to fix it. Even though she had a successful career, she did not let the success that she'd achieved keep her from pivoting to stay true to her own authentic purpose path.

Perhaps you, like Carolyn, have attained a great position of influence or prestige, or have carved out a stable career path for yourself, but you feel a real sense of restlessness by being in the wrong role. It takes a special courage to take what appears to be a step back in order to take a step forward to do what you're truly called to do with your life. It's never too late. When you have been given the gift of clarity that you need to walk away from your path of least resistance, will you have the courage to follow your calling?

Vocational Courage: Mind-Set and Habit

Many of us come to a point in our lives where we reach a crossroads, a place where the pathway leading to our future self diverges. We have a choice to make: to continue traveling along the path we're on or to take another path altogether. Some of us reach this crossroads early in our lives, while we're in high school or soon after we graduate from college. Others of us reach it much later in life; there's a reason why the familiar condition known as a *midlife crisis,* which I discussed in chapter 4, has earned that name. The point is that you never know when you will gain clarity on your calling.

The question for most of us when we get to that place in our life and career is, "Which path should I take, and will I have the courage necessary to make the right choice when I am called?"

Researchers have invested no small amount of time examining the choices people make—or don't make—when confronted with decisions about work and careers. According to a report published by Mental Health America and the Faas Foundation, the vast majority of American workers are dissatisfied with their current jobs—so much so that 71 percent reported they were looking to change employers.[1]

Based on this overwhelming number of people who want to change the trajectory of their careers and their lives, you might think that a large portion of this cohort would follow through with their wish. But according to data published by the U.S. Bureau of Labor Statistics in its Current Population Survey, only about 6.2 million workers from 2015 to 2016—or just 4 percent of the total workforce—transferred from one occupational group to another.[2]

Why the gap between people who want to change their careers—perhaps onto a path that is better aligned with what they are called to do—and those who actually do it? I believe there are three main reasons.

First, many people allow inertia to create an obstacle between the vocation they dream of and the job they do. While change is constant in the world around us, we humans tend to prefer the safety of the routine and the predictable— and perhaps even the boring. In a 2017 study, researchers Ed O'Brien and Nadav Klein of the University of Chicago found that people naturally tend to believe failure is a more likely outcome than success.[3] This belief, erroneous or not, biases people to avoid change and prefer the status quo. Whether the inertia that keeps us firmly planted in the status quo derives from the expectations of our parents or loved ones, or from the socialization we have experienced academically or professionally, its power over us cannot be overestimated.

Second, for financial and other reasons, some people simply don't have a reasonable choice to leave one career behind and embark on an entirely new one. If you depend on your job for the income and benefits you need to keep you and your family afloat, then turning your back on the security it provides may be a luxury that you just can't afford—at least not until you are on a firmer financial footing. In addition, it may take time to gather and hone the skills or the additional education required to do well in pursuing your life's work. If this is the case, then you may need to focus on preparing while you (temporarily) stay in a job that isn't aligned with your calling. After all, the call to pursue your life's work is really first a call to preparation first.

Third, many people simply lack the courage required to step out of a job that isn't aligned with what they are called to do, and to step into a job that is. Make no mistake about it—trading a successful career for a more uncertain path that could very well fail takes a tremendous amount of courage, even when that new path is fully aligned with what you have been called to do.

PROFILE IN COURAGE: *Marsha Smith*

Little Rock native Marsha Smith joined a global media company fresh out of college, ready to carve out a prosperous career for herself in the client services business. Within the first decade of her career, she rose through the ranks quickly to the vice-president level and couldn't help but notice that she was the only African American vice president in the entire company. She saw the task of correcting the lack of diversity in her company as akin to the task of the Greek mythological figure Sisyphus, whose task it was to roll an enormous boulder uphill, only for it to roll back down as it neared the top. Despite the seemingly improbable odds of success, Marsha knew in her gut that this would be a Sisyphean task, that this was her boulder.

Since reaching that conclusion, Marsha has shifted gears and taken on leadership of her company's diversity and inclusion initiatives in the workplace and marketplace and assumed a critical leadership role in the industry.

As Brené Brown, a research professor at the University of Houston, suggests, we have two choices when we are faced with a pivotal situation such as this: "We can choose to respond from fear or we can choose courage."[4] Fear is the great paralyzer, and while it comes from a very real place within our minds—often based in our life experiences or the experiences of others around us—it does us no good when we are trying to align our career with our calling. Courage moves us forward, while fear holds us back.

According to Brené Brown, when we demonstrate courage in what we do, our actions ripple out to those around us. Says Brown, "Courage is contagious. Every time we choose courage, we make everyone around us a little better and the world a little braver."[5] When you choose to be vocationally courageous, others will be inspired by your example and build the courage they need to align themselves with *their* calling.

When you're confronted with clarity regarding what your vocation is, courage is demonstrated by actually doing the alignment work to make sure that what you're doing every day is consistent with your calling, whatever it may be. Demonstrating vocational courage is both a mind-set and a habit. It's more than a single decision: it's a daily commitment to invest your time and your talent and energy in ways that facilitate the accomplishment of your life's work. For most people, this will involve making courageous choices regarding what they do every day.

Vocational courage shows up in different ways for different people, depending on their circumstances. For some people, the vocationally courageous thing to do is to focus on taking care of their families and loved ones while putting their own personal ambition or pursuit of deeper self-actualization on hold. I personally know people who have put their plans to finish college degrees on hold or who have made the difficult (but courageous) decision to turn down lucrative job offers that would take them away from their families because they had to do what they believed was best for their families at the time.

There are people around the world who are making difficult decisions to put their own dreams on hold because they believe that the best and highest use of themselves in the world at the moment is to provide love and support to an aging parent, a seriously ill spouse, or a house full of active, growing children. They choose to do whatever they need to do to put food on the table for their families and to be able to spend the quality and quantity of time with them that is necessary. While it may appear that they're not pursuing their life's work at the time, they're demonstrating a special type of vocational courage that places career as secondary to purpose.

Vocational courage is much more than engaging in risk-seeking behavior. There are plenty of books available on the topics of entrepreneurship, on courageous decision-making, and on career navigation and starting up your own business and being your own CEO. That's not what vocational courage is: it's not professional risk-seeking for its own sake.

Vocational courage is about taking the risk that you cannot afford *not* to take in order to be able to look at yourself in the mirror with a sense of satisfaction and fulfillment. Ultimately, that's where courage comes in.

And vocational courage is not simply required in determining one's vocation and path in life. Hearing God's voice clearly through the din of others' voices is sometimes a courageous act in itself, to help you focus and gain that clarity. However, courage is mainly needed in committing to act on the calling you receive. Remember Parker Palmer's words about his understanding of vocation "not as a goal to be achieved but as a gift to be received."[6] If vocation is in fact a gift to be received, then the courage is in making the difficult and often counterintuitive decisions that are necessary to align your daily work with your life's work.

There are many voices telling us why making this alignment is not a good idea or even impossible. There are the voices in your own head that tell you you're not smart enough, or you're not rich enough, or you're not old enough, or you're too old, or any number of other excuses. There are the voices of a spouse or loved one, warning you that you're putting your family's standard of living at some risk, or that you're being self-centered or selfish. And there may be the voice of a mentor, telling you that no one's successfully done that before, or simply, "I tried that and it didn't work."

All of these voices weigh heavily on one's mind and can provide numerous reasons for why you *shouldn't* align your work with your calling. True courage is in listening to what these (perhaps) well-meaning people have to say, learning from their experience and even from their warnings, but then overcoming all the reasons why you shouldn't pursue what you have been called to do. It requires profound clarity and deep courage to overcome the pure inertia of what already is. With courage lifting you up, you'll be able to accomplish not only what could be, but what *must* be.

The Time Is Now

As I wrote this book, I wanted to be absolutely clear that the kinds of career shifts that require vocational courage can arrive on our doorstep at most any time of life and are not limited to the proverbial midlife crisis or any other particular time.

When we were children, I suspect each one of us could quickly summon an answer when asked, "What do you want to be when you grow up?" Chances are, few of us became the doctors or firefighters or princesses or secret agents that we imagined we would be when we looked to the distant future of our adulthood.

And for those of us who attended college, there's a good chance we entered school with a particular career path (or two) in mind—and a major to go along with that path—but then both career and major were discarded as we were exposed to new ideas, new possibilities, and new opportunities. While you might have started out as a premed, biology major, fully committed to becoming a physician, you may have graduated as a business or economics major (the National Center for Education Statistics reports that approximately one-third of US college students in bachelor's degree programs changed their major at least once within three years of their initial enrollment).[7] And then, after you graduated and began the job search, you might have transitioned into an entirely different career—much as I became a pastor, business school professor, and consultant instead of the chemical engineer I trained in college to be.

Which brings us back to what happens when we reach middle age, a time when many of us experience, if not a midlife crisis, at least midlife doldrums—a sense that we aren't engaged in work that has a purpose, and that time is quickly ticking by.

According to a study conducted by the Happiness Research Institute in Copenhagen, Denmark, the number-one source of professional contentment is having a sense of purpose.[8] This desire to connect work with purpose comes to a head when we enter middle age—a time when we naturally look back over what we have accomplished and assess whether or not we have made a difference in the world around us. Says Philip Pizzo of Stanford University's Distinguished Careers Institute, "When people get to their mid-career phase, they want to give back and do something meaningful."[9]

I personally believe that we all want to do work that is meaningful at every stage of our lives: we long to live lives of purpose. In addition, there is evidence that living a life with purpose has medical as well as psychological benefits. According to a study by researchers at Rush University Medical Center in Chicago, people whose brains show the physical damage of Alzheimer's disease, but who feel strongly that they have a purpose in life, are two and a half times less likely to suffer memory loss and other symptoms of the disease.[10]

The best time to align your work with your calling is when you become aware that you have been called. And if you have not yet acted, then the time is *now*. Responding to the call may require you to be courageous and to overcome the fear you may feel about embarking on a career path that might not offer the comfort and familiarity of what you are doing now. But by aligning yourself with what you are meant to do, your life will have purpose and meaning.

The One Thing You Can't *Not* Do

But where does one go to find courage when it can't be found?

What if I don't feel courageous? What if I'm scared and anxious about changing the path I'm on? What if the thought of making a transition from one career to another makes me afraid? What if it makes my spouse or those close to me afraid?

Nelson Mandela, a courageous individual if ever there was one, once said, "I learned that courage was not the absence of fear, but the triumph over it. The brave man is not he who does not feel afraid, but he who conquers that fear."[11]

Vocational courage is not the absence of fear, it is looking at all the reasons why you should not follow your calling in life and coming to the realization that you must do it anyway. Not necessarily because you want to or because you think it's a good idea, but because you simply can't *not* do it. It isn't coming up with a career path that is "cool" or "fun" or that satisfies your ego or even that makes you happy. It's the realization that if you don't take the leap to do what you are called to do, you will never be able to realize the upside, you will never be able to fulfill the destiny your Creator made for you and only you. It's coming to terms with the fact that you will not have rest unless and until you do this.

In 1 Corinthians 9:16, Paul says, "For if I preach the gospel, I have nothing to boast of, for necessity is laid upon me; yes, woe is me if I do not preach the gospel!"[12] It is necessary for me. It is something that I cannot *not* do. There's an inner compulsion that comes from this—if I don't do it, I'm actually going to be worse off than if I do it and all the circumstances don't work out quite as I had hoped.

So, ultimately, if you don't *feel* courageous in pursuing your calling, that's okay. This is not about a feeling at all. This is about a mandate that you cannot *not* fulfill—you can't afford to not do this. Try as you might, it's harder for you to resist the calling than it is for you to live with the difficulties and obstacles that may very well arise.

That's not to say courage is not required; it absolutely is, because there are things you have to overcome as you travel the pathway laid out by your Creator. You have to get your mind right; just because you are called to a particular work doesn't mean that God forces your will to shift. There are people throughout history who have tried not to do what they were called to do. In an earlier chapter I mentioned the example of Jeremiah, who was called by God to be a prophet. Jeremiah knew what he was called to do, but it got difficult and he wanted to quit. According to Jeremiah 20:9:

> *Then I said, "I will not make mention of Him, nor speak anymore in His name." But His word was in my heart like a burning fire shut up in my bones; I was weary of holding it back, and I could not.*[13]

Your true vocation may be like a burning fire shut up in your bones, and great courage is required not to extinguish the fire. It takes courage to overcome the voices that say you shouldn't follow the path laid out for you, and it takes courage to overcome your own self-doubts.

In Exodus, after God called Moses to lead the children of Israel out of Egypt, Moses vigorously expressed his self-doubts to God. According to Exodus 4:10:

> *Then Moses said to the Lord, "O my Lord, I am not eloquent, neither before nor since You have spoken to Your servant; but I am slow of speech and slow of tongue."*[14]

God demanded Moses' obedience, explaining that Moses' brother Aaron would speak the words that God had spoken to Moses. Moses relented, taking the rod of God in his hand. It took great courage for Moses to accept God's calling and to take on the monumental task of leading the Israelites to the Promised Land. And he did.

Living a Faithful Life

Many reluctant people ultimately recognize that it is their obedience that God desires most, not their ability to work through all the details. What God is looking for—what God expects—is faithfulness in the moment of decision, and obedience to what you have received from God. Thus, if God places it before you, God will make the necessary provision. If God provides the vision, then God will also provide the provision.

If God has given you clear instruction around what your life's work is and what He would have you do, and you can't add up all the numbers and make all the facts and figures and dates and times work out in your brain, that should not greatly concern you. It's up to you to take one step in faith—one step at a time, one day at a time—not understand the entire staircase or where it leads. You should not expect to be able to make the grand pronouncement, "Here is my life's work in full, crystal-clear detail, fifty or sixty years in advance." Instead, your life's work is an unfolding picture that is revealed over years and even decades. My hope is that you will have the courage to be obedient to the part that has been revealed to you by God, in the absence of the rest of the story.

Many people think that if they don't have a plan—a road map for their life—one that outlines every step they should take, they can't and shouldn't proceed. I believe you don't need to have a complete plan; what you need to have is a *yes*.

I push back against the idea of people having ten- or twenty-year plans for their lives and their careers. It's a beautiful idea, but it's just not realistic when you're trying to live in a way that is completely sensitive to the voice of God. When I was in college, one of my advisors was trying to get us to make long-term plans for career and life because, as he liked to say, "When you fail to plan, you plan to fail." I took a lot of that to heart, but then I looked back at my own path and recognized that what God has rewarded in my short life was not my command of all the details, but my willingness to say, "If you send me, I'll go. If this is where you want me to go, then I trust that you will work out the details." I realized that whatever I might have lost from not overmanaging my life's path was worthless in comparison to what I gained by being faithful in each moment.

Nothing catches God by surprise. When you decide whether or not to answer the call of your Maker, it fundamentally comes down to a question of whether or not you trust God. God is faithful. God has never failed. God has not been caught by surprise once, even when the details don't add up in our brains. Our cognition and our ability to process God's ways are finite and imperfect. When we refuse to move forward and demand to have everything figured out despite knowing what God has already led us to do, it suggests that we want to be God and do not trust Him. God's ways are higher than ours, His thoughts are higher than ours, thus our feeble human attempts to understand God, and fit Him into a box of human reasoning and logic before we take action on what God has led us to do are flawed at best.

There are days when we will get it wrong, but the next day you wake up to a new chance to get it right. Faithfulness isn't perfection—it is about the tendency and inclination of your heart, mind, and behavior. It is the narrative arc of your heart. The Reverend Dr. Martin Luther King, Jr., often paraphrased a mid-nineteenth-century sermon by Transcendentalist reformer and abolitionist the Rev. Theodore Parker, saying, "The arc of the moral universe is long, but it bends toward justice." From the perspective of vocational courage, may it be said for each of us that the arc of our lives was long, but it bent toward faithfully pleasing God.

That is vocational courage. That is courageous faithful living. Yes, you may sometimes feel like you're taking one step forward and two steps backward, but when you zoom out and take a look at your life as a whole, you can see that it was actually two or three steps forward and one step back. There were ups and there were surely downs, but the overall trend was upward. That's why this is a life's work, not just a career decision. Although your life's work includes career decisions, they alone do not tell the full story in isolation from the rest of the narrative.

Keep in mind that there may be a time when you are called in a different direction, as the full story of your life is revealed. It will be just as courageous of you to pivot and pursue that new direction as it was for you to pivot the first time and pursue what you're doing today. This can be a difficult concept to grasp because we tend to want to think about life's work and career as being structurally equivalent— that if we're in a particular career it must be the right one.

The reality is that you may be called by God to a new season of your life, asking and requiring you to be faithful in a different way. Faithfulness takes a different look.

The challenge comes when people equate their activities with their vocation. Vocation and activity or job or career are very different things. I have one vocation that gets lived out on multiple platforms—minister, professor, and executive advisor. There will come a time where perhaps one of these platforms will occupy less space in my life or perhaps no longer be a part of it at all. I have to be okay with that. My understanding of my life's work is broad enough to encompass occupying different platforms. When God calls, I will say "Yes." Always.

Stewarding Your Vocation

Within the last year, I was presented with an opportunity that required me to once again listen closely to God's calling and then draw from my personal reservoir of vocational courage. More about that in just a bit.

Each of us is presented with all sorts of career and other opportunities during the course of our lives. While it's often easy to just say "Yes" to them as they arise, if we aren't careful, these opportunities may take us off the path of what it is we are meant to do with our lives.

In chapter 3, I described how I built a career hybrid that was uniquely mine—serving as a professor, pastor, and executive consultant. While on the surface these three distinct careers may seem disconnected, I personally consider them to be a single vocation that plays out on different platforms—allowing me to do the work I am uniquely called to do.

You have the ability and power to express yourself and your vocation in many different ways. If you are a consultant, for example, you can work directly with clients or you can blog, write a book or magazine articles, conduct workshop seminars and webinars, or create podcasts or YouTube videos. There are many ways for you to get your ideas and recommendations and advice out to the world to help others. But when you are presented with opportunities to express your vocation on different platforms, how do you decide which ones you should embrace and which ones you should turn down?

When you find yourself presented with these kinds of choices, it is not so much about finding the courage to align yourself vocationally, but instead finding the courage required to steward your vocation well. The courage comes not only when I ask myself, "What am I saying yes to?" but also when I ask, "What am I saying no to?" If I am being faithful to the path my Creator has laid out for my life, I will not only do it, but I will do it on God's terms. I don't control the *when*, I don't control the *where*, I don't control the *how*, and I don't control the *who* in terms of the audience. None of that is under my control.

As I said at the beginning of this section, I was called again by my Creator within the past year. For many years,

I knew since studying at Harvard Divinity School as an undergraduate religious-studies concentrator that completing my master's degree in theology was part of God's plan for me, though I did not know exactly when and how it would fit into my overstuffed life. Yet, in the past year, I was presented with the opportunity to attend seminary to complete that very degree. This came in addition to the three different career paths on which I am currently traveling, along with the arrival of our first child in fall 2017. You probably won't be surprised to learn that, when I received this calling, I asked God, "Why now?" And when I asked my Creator that question, it became abundantly clear to me that this was the time.

Why seminary *now*? Because God said so.

Why earn my PhD and become a professor at Northwestern *before* pursuing a master's degree in theology? Because it is preparatory for the work I am supposed to do.

There is, of course, an element of human decision-making in everything I do in my life, but I would hope—and I think the choices I have made thus far have borne this out—that I have succeeded at least to some degree in my feeble attempt to try to do God's will for me at this moment. Complicated though it may be, inconvenient though it may be, uncomfortable though it may be, in sum it is joyous to me.

Making this decision required clarity around this being a step that was in service of my life's work. God was clear with me in no uncertain terms that this was the time. My bargaining and negotiating with God over timing and place and all of those details was irrelevant. My decision was either to say "Yes" and let God work it out, or say "No" and face the consequences of disobedience.

I said "Yes," and God is working it out.

7

Rechecking Your Alignment

Only when your intent and actions are in alignment can you create the reality you desire.

—STEVE MARABOLI

While I don't personally know what Michelle Obama dreamed of being when she grew up, I suspect that First Lady of the United States probably wasn't at the top of her to-do list. First of all, when she was born in 1964, the fight for civil rights in the United States was in full swing and the possibility that an African American president would one day be elected seemed remote—perhaps impossible in our lifetime. Second, she had other plans for her life—plans that were revised and realigned numerous times as she listened to the calling of her God.

Michelle LaVaughn Robinson was born and raised in Chicago, and she grew up in a one-bedroom, one-bathroom apartment with her father, Fraser—who worked for the Chicago water department as a pump operator despite living since the age of thirty with the tremendous physical challenge of multiple sclerosis—her mother, Marian, and older brother, Craig. According to Michelle Obama, "My father was a blue-collar worker. . . . My mother stayed home to raise me and my brother. We were the first to graduate from college in our immediate family."[1] Her family attended worship services at South Shore United Methodist Church, just a couple of blocks away from her home.

Early on, Michelle was a standout in school. She skipped second grade at the segregated Bryn Mawr Elementary School (since renamed the Bouchet Mathematics & Science Academy) and she was named salutatorian of her graduating class at our shared alma mater, Whitney M. Young Magnet High School—Chicago's first public magnet high school. It was here that she took the Advanced Placement classes that would help propel her to an offer of admissions from Princeton University, where she enrolled in 1981 (and where her brother, Craig, had enrolled two years prior).

When Michelle started at Princeton, she had set her sights on becoming a physician, but those plans quickly changed. Says Obama, "I wanted to be a pediatrician, until I realized science wasn't much fun."[2] She felt out of place at Princeton—the rare black student in a very conservative and predominantly white Ivy League institution—and the mother of her white college roommate reportedly demanded that her daughter be moved to a different room. To its credit, the university refused her demands. Michelle went on to major in sociology with a minor in African

American studies, and she graduated with a bachelor of arts degree cum laude.

Instead of going on to a career in some sociology-related field—perhaps as a social worker or community advocate or rehabilitation counselor—Michelle made another pivotal decision in her life: she chose to attend law school and become an attorney. She was accepted by Harvard Law School and graduated with her JD degree in 1988. While at Harvard, Michelle served the community by helping low-income clients navigate housing issues as a volunteer at the student-run Harvard Legal Aid Bureau, and for some time she edited the *BlackLetter Law Journal*, a publication of Harvard's Black Law Students Association.

After graduating from Harvard Law School, Michelle made the decision to practice corporate law, and she accepted a position at the high-powered Chicago-based law firm Sidley Austin. It was here that she would meet her future husband, Barack Obama, a summer associate whom she was assigned to mentor. Although she remained at the firm for three years, she knew something was wrong: her purpose and her chosen career were out of alignment. Reflecting back on her decision to pursue a career in corporate law, Obama explains that her Harvard experience naturally pushed her in that direction—perhaps so loudly and so persistently that the voice of her Caller was drowned out. Says Obama:

The thing about these wonderful schools is they can be surprisingly narrowing to your perspective. You can be a lawyer or you can work on Wall Street; those are the conventional options. They're easy, socially acceptable, and financially rewarding. Why wouldn't you do it?[3]

Michelle left Sidley Austin in 1991 to pursue opportunities that would be in better alignment with her purpose. In an interview, a partner at Sidley Austin—Quincy White, who was instrumental in recruiting Michelle to the firm— offers his assessment of why she left. Says White, "I couldn't give her something that would meet her sense of ambition to change the world."[4] And if anything, Michelle was driven by a strong desire to change the world.

According to her profile on the White House website, "After a few years, Mrs. Obama decided her true calling was working with people to serve their communities and their neighbors." During the next few years, Michelle worked in a variety of different positions—an assistant to Chicago mayor Richard M. Daley, assistant commissioner of planning and development for the City of Chicago, and the founding executive director of the Chicago chapter of Public Allies—preparing young people for careers in public service. Says Michelle about her time at Public Allies, which she built within two years into an organization with a $1.1 million annual budget, mentoring up to forty clients a year, "I was never happier in my life than when I was working to build Public Allies."[5] She and Barack Obama were married in 1992.

In 1996, Michelle accepted a position as associate dean of Student Services at the University of Chicago—charged with building connections between the greater Chicago community and the university. While in that position, she founded the University Community Service Center (UCSC), which, according to the organization's website:

> *prepares students to become productive, thoughtful citizens and effective, inspiring leaders in their communities and professions by providing them with service and social change opportunities that complement UChicago's rigorous academic experience.*[6]

She eventually migrated over to the University of Chicago Medical Center, in 2002 accepting a position as executive director for community affairs, and in 2005 becoming the organization's vice president of the Office of Community and External Affairs. Her work at the University of Chicago Medical Center brought her high school ambition to pursue a career in medicine back into her life, if only in an administrative role.

In the meantime, in addition to his career as a civil rights attorney and professor at the University of Chicago School of Law, Michelle's husband, Barack, decided to pursue political office—creating a hybrid career closely aligned with his purpose. He was elected to the Illinois Senate in 1996, where he served through 2004 (while still working as an attorney and professor), and he was elected to the United States Senate in 2004. In 2008 he was elected the forty-fourth president of the United States.

Mrs. Obama was First Lady of the United States throughout her husband Barack Obama's two terms in office, from January 2009 through January 2017. During this time, she led four major programs: Let's Move!, launched in 2010, which brought together parents, medical professionals, community leaders, and educators to address the problem of childhood obesity within a generation; Joining Forces, launched with Dr. Jill Biden in 2011, which called on Americans to support service members, their families, and veterans in securing opportunities in education, employment, and wellness; Reach Higher Initiative, launched in 2014 with the goal of encouraging young people to complete an education beyond high school—in a professional training program, community college, or four-year college or university; and Let Girls Learn, a 2015 initiative aimed at encouraging and aiding girls to attend and stay in school.[7]

As First Lady, Michelle Obama had a unique opportunity to closely align her purpose with her daily work—making a tremendous difference on people's lives across the nation and around the world. All because she was willing to listen to the voice of her Caller and then follow His direction. As she said in a 2007 South Carolina speech:

When I listened to my own voice and cast the cynics aside, when I forged ahead and overcame the doubts and fears of others about who I was and what I could become, I found that their doubts and fears were misplaced. Funny thing, the more I achieved, the more I found that I was just as ready, just as qualified, just as capable as those who felt entitled to the seat at the table that I was working so hard for. And I realized that those who had been given the mantle of power in this country didn't have any magic about them. They were no better, no smarter than me. That gnawing sense of self-doubt that is common within all of us is a lie. It's just in our heads. Nine times out of ten, we are more ready and more prepared than we could ever know.[8]

Change Happens

A vocation is not something that we can set and forget; it requires periodic checks to ensure that the path on which we are walking is still aligned with our calling. As I briefly mentioned in the previous chapter, our understanding of our calling can evolve over time—gaining greater dimension, depth, and breadth as we evolve and as we experience more of what life has to offer.

As your understanding of vocation grows, so too must your responsibility for stewarding your vocation. To whom much is given, much is required. So if you have been given a little clarity, then you are responsible for stewarding that: you're ultimately responsible for what you do with this knowledge. Happiness, fulfillment, meaning, and passion all come from this.

PROFILE IN COURAGE: *Mark Pawloski*

One of my former students, SoFi Entrepreneur Program member Mark Pawloski, started his career with a lucrative job in the banking world, but he soon left the amazing compensation behind to create impact—as an educator with Teach for America and then for charter schools and after-schooltime nonprofits. Frustrated by what he witnessed in the education sector, he decided to marry his background in banking with his passion for education reform. Instead of taking the safe road, Mark launched himself into entrepreneurship and cofounded Upkey, a "student incubator that helps connect . . . students with potential employers."[9]

Rechecking that you are aligned with your calling requires getting in touch with your Maker. But what if your connection is fuzzy, or what if you feel like you're no longer in contact with Him?

I like to think about this situation in much the same way as being in a conversation with someone on a mobile phone and the connection fades in and out or gets cut off. This happens to me all the time when I'm talking to my wife after a long day at work. Invariably, she will walk into a tunnel or get on an elevator, or I will drive through a dead zone on the expressway, and the communication gets interrupted. When this happens, it does not mean that my wife or I have stopped speaking. It just means that the connection is weak or cut off because we have gone out of range of the phone signal.

If you embark on the process of rechecking your alignment and you can no longer hear the voice of your Caller, it's not because the Caller has stopped speaking. Your Caller is God, and sometimes we can no longer hear His voice because we have gone into places where we have moved out of the range and cut ourselves off from hearing His voice. He's still speaking, but we're not hearing.

How does this happen?

It happens when we are no longer in a position to receive. It could be because we feel completely self-sufficient and believe we no longer need God's help, or because we are comfortable right where we are and no longer listen to the voice of our Caller. Comfort is a complacent feeling in which you're settled in and satisfied with the status quo. Comfort is a place where you rest on your laurels and enjoy the ride. Comfort is a place where you cling tightly to your career because you and your career and the perception of your professional success are intertwined.

But the call of God is to care more about being faithful

to Him than to a prescribed career trajectory. Some people cling so tightly to their careers and the applause that comes with success that they miss the voice of their vocation. As a result, they begin to get absorbed in *what* they're doing, not *why* they're doing it. Vocation is far more about a greater *why* than it is about a particular *what,* because the what will shift with time. It has to.

After earning his MBA at the Kellogg School of Management in 1991, John Wood accepted a position at Microsoft, where he served as an executive, including positions as director of business development for Greater China, director of marketing for Australia, and director of marketing for the Asia-Pacific region. While Wood was on the fast track for success at Microsoft, he knew something wasn't right. The technology industry was growing by leaps and bounds during the 1990s, and according to Wood, "the only way to keep up was to work crazy hours."[10] His life was increasingly dominated by stress and pressure to perform.

After seven years of the crazy hours—and constantly flying to meetings all around the globe—Wood's relationships with family and friends deteriorated, and some crumbled entirely. He began to wonder if it was all worth it. Says Wood in his book *Leaving Microsoft to Change the World*:

> *Seven years in, though, that nagging question continually popped up: Is this all there is—longer hours*

and bigger payoffs? I had adopted the commando lifestyle of a corporate warrior. Vacation was for people who were soft. Real players worked weekends, racked up hundreds of thousands of air miles, and built mini-empires within the expanding global colossus called Microsoft. Complainers simply did not care about the company's future.[11]

After a particularly tumultuous set of business-review meetings with Steve Ballmer, Microsoft's president at the time (which were said to typically involve much shouting and haranguing), in 1998 Wood and a colleague decided to take a much-needed, three-week trekking vacation in Nepal. They would hike the two hundred miles along the challenging Annapurna Circuit, reaching altitudes higher than seventeen thousand feet and mentally and physically remove themselves just about as far away as they could from the hard-charging Microsoft culture.

During the course of the trek, after a particularly difficult ascent, Wood and his companions arrived in a village, Bahundanda, where they visited a school. The school was packed with 450 students divided into eight classrooms. The trekkers met the headmaster of the school, who led them to the school library. According to Wood, there were no books in the library. When he asked the headmaster where the books were, he unlocked the cabinet where the books were kept. Says Wood:

The headmaster explained. Books were considered precious. The school had so few that the teachers did not want to risk the children damaging them. I wondered how a book could impart knowledge if it was locked up, but kept that thought to myself.[12]

Concerned that the students were being deprived of such a basic thing as a book, but not wanting to insult his host, Wood wondered what he could do to help. He received his answer when the headmaster suggested, "Perhaps, sir, you will someday come back with books."

One year later, Wood returned to Bahundanda with three thousand books donated by family and friends, and when he returned to the United States, he resigned from his executive position at Microsoft. Thus was born Room to Read, a nonprofit cofounded by Wood, Dinesh Shrestha, and Erin Ganju.

Says Wood about his decision to leave behind his lucrative corporate job to start up a nonprofit organization with no guarantee of success, but which would align him with his purpose:

One library is a drop in the ocean in the world of 780 million people who are illiterate. I faced a dilemma—I could go back to Microsoft where I was in charge of business development for Greater China, and I could make Room to Read my hobby. But the problem is hobbies don't scale. I wanted to do this in a big way—go big or go home. I'd have to quit my job and do it full time. I literally threw myself off the Microsoft plane and prayed the parachute would deploy.[13]

In the years since Wood made his first trek through the towering mountains of Nepal, Room to Read has distributed more than twenty million books, trained almost nine thousand teachers and librarians, partnered with more than 19,500 schools, and benefited more than ten million children through its literacy programs. In addition, the organization's Girls' Education Program has enrolled more than forty-seven thousand girls with a dropout rate of just 6 percent.[14]

In his book *Purpose, Incorporated,* Wood suggests that the classic four Ps of marketing—product, price, promotion, and placement—have recently been joined by a fifth P—purpose. He describes how companies large and small have begun to use a sense of corporate purpose as a competitive advantage to win new customers and differentiate themselves in the marketplace.

And while customers get excited when they find a company that they share a purpose with, so too do employees—and prospective employees. This is especially the case for millennials. According to a study conducted by Cone, Inc., and AMP Agency, 79 percent of millennials surveyed report that they want to work for employers that care about how they impact/contribute to society, and 44 percent said they would actively pursue working for a company after learning about its social commitment.[15]

Just as it's important for people to align closely with their purpose, so too is it important for organizations to align with *their* purpose. More on that in chapter 9.

Approaching a Transition Zone

Falling out of alignment with your calling doesn't typically happen all at once. It happens in stages, one small step at a time, until you approach a transition zone—a pivotal time in your career and life. Depending on the choices you make as you enter, navigate, and then exit the transition zone, you may more closely align with your calling or you may find yourself further from it than ever.

But how can you tell that you might be approaching a transition zone? One sure sign is a restlessness that you might feel—a feeling that whatever career you may be engaged in, it isn't where you belong. You don't feel like you're in the right place or the right role. You might feel that the impact you're making on the world around you is insufficient or not channeled in the right direction. You might also have a feeling that you have been successful by someone else's standards—your parents', your spouse's, your boss's—but you can see that the "success" you've achieved is meaningless compared to what you know you were created to do.

In a *Forbes* article, Philippe Gaud—an affiliate professor at HEC Paris—tells the story about how in his mid-fifties he decided to pivot from a twenty-five-year career as a human resources executive for high-profile, international companies, to teaching. Says Gaud, "I had no real reason to abandon a career that was developing very well. No real reason, that is, except one, crucial one. I wanted something different."[16] While he doesn't explicitly say it, I would guess that Gaud had been called to this new career for some time, and it became so loud and so insistent that he couldn't *not* do it.

According to Gaud, there are several ways to help ensure that you successfully make it through the transition zone. One is to consider making a major career change when you are at the pinnacle of your career. This might seem counterintuitive, but Gaud says when you're at the top of your game, "your all-important self-confidence will be at its strongest, you're upbeat and ready to tackle new challenges."

Gaud also warns that your primary motivation shouldn't be trying to escape a bad or unsatisfying work situation. I couldn't agree more. You should be drawn to an opportunity because it is better aligned with the vocation that God has uniquely designed you for. Moreover, as Gaud points out, sometimes we put on blinders, looking only at career opportunities within the organizations at which we currently work. He suggests that it's important to look outward as well, keeping an eye out for opportunities that might arise outside of your current company or context.

When is the right time in one's life to make a change? There's no particular age, says Gaud. It's time "when you can't answer the question: what did I learn today?" Ultimately, when it's time to go, it's time to go. Instead of dragging your feet and hemming and hawing, when God lights the path of a new course for you, your job is to just go. Hear His voice calling you, trust Him and His plan for your life. Make the leap in faith, knowing that God will work out the details as you follow His direction.

There's certainly a degree of impatience that many people talk about when it comes to, for example, millennials wanting to be promoted quickly into jobs of greater importance or with greater impact. And in the case of millennials, this youthful impatience can be quite real. According to a Gallup report titled *Millennials: The Job-Hopping Generation,* the belief that millennials—people born between 1980 and 1996—are less tied to their jobs and companies than other generations is generally an accurate one. The report reveals that "21 percent of millennials say they've changed jobs within the past year, which is more than three times the number of non-millennials who report the same." In addition, 60 percent of millennials report that they are open to new job opportunities.[17] But youthful impatience is not the same as the restlessness you might feel that the career you have chosen or the job you have accepted is not where you belong.

What's missing for many of us is taking the time to be still, to find a quiet place to contemplate and to listen for the voice of our Creator. Many of us are addicted to busyness and the feeling of being overwhelmed. There is almost a cultural value that prizes being busy even more than being productive. In the face of such overwhelming levels of busyness and the stress that comes along with it, we are less mindful and less reflective. We try to cope with this busyness and stress by going on autopilot—taking time- and effort-saving mental shortcuts to navigate our day-to-day lives.

Such mental shortcuts are called *heuristics*—"simple, efficient rules which people often use to form judgments and make decisions."[18] However, these shortcuts—educated guesses, rules of thumb, intuitive feelings—can lead to cognitive biases that do not work in our favor, nor in the favor of those around us.

Take the April 2018 example of two African American men who were arrested in a Philadelphia Starbucks. Starbucks, as a company, has long promoted itself as a neighborhood meeting place and a workspace away from the office. I imagine that millions of informal business meetings have taken place in all the Starbucks stores around the world. Of course, the company hopes that you will buy a coffee or two and perhaps some food while you're occupying their space, but there's no formal companywide policy that says this has to be the case.

When the two black men (who were waiting to meet a

white business colleague) told the store manager they were not interested in purchasing anything, police were called and the two men were arrested and held for more than six hours before they were released with no charges filed. When the incident blew up in the media, Starbucks CEO Kevin Johnson made many public apologies—and apologies to the two men who were arrested—explaining that the company's employees erred in calling the police, inferring that their unconscious bias was to blame.

In the United States, some people unconsciously make the implicit racial association between black and bad, and white and good—black threatening, white good. Of course, in reality, such heuristics have no basis in fact, and they have led to tragic consequences—namely the tragic and senseless loss of black lives. These are the kinds of mental shortcuts we can't afford to take.

Have You Missed Your Exit?

Similarly, I would argue that being on autopilot in terms of our daily work and being successful and being praised and applauded is a shortcut we can't afford to take, either. Just because someone else is applauding you for the work you do and calling you a success does not mean that you are doing what you are uniquely designed to do at this time of your life. In fact, it's quite possible that you are not—especially if you have not been in touch with your Maker lately.

The leaders I've spoken with—including recently North-western University Kellogg School of Management's Sally Blount, as she approached the end of her almost decade-long tenure as dean—confirm that there comes a very deep sense of knowing when it is time to transition. In almost every case, it's better to do it on your own terms—with you in charge of where you'll go and when. But some people become comfortable where they are, and they overstay their welcome.

In September 2017, Sally announced that she would step down from her post as dean at the end of the 2017–2018 academic year—deciding that it was time to exit this chapter of her career on her terms and on her schedule. According to the announcement, Blount launched four key strategic initiatives during her tenure as dean. She also led Kellogg's Transforming Together campaign, which raised $350 million (surpassing the previous fund-raising record for the school by $15 million) and presided over fund-raising for the Kellogg Global Hub, a new 415,000-square-foot building for the school, which opened in 2017.[19]

By every measure, Blount was at the top of her game when she decided to take the exit ramp from her tenure as dean of the Kellogg School. But during a silent retreat in Rhode Island in the summer of 2017, Blount rechecked her alignment and she heard the voice of her Caller loud and clear. Says Blount about her decision and the vocational courage that was required to make it:

While on retreat in July, I realized that this inflection point creates an opportunity for me to start thinking bravely about my own life in the ways that I have about the institutions I have led. I have long dreamed of taking a sabbatical year to travel, to write, and I want to spend some time thinking about my own final chapter in education as the pace of transformation accelerates in our workplace. As my daughter once said to me long ago, "This is what the person I want to become would do."[20]

In a *Forbes* article, Blount explains that when you do make the decision to exit from a career, the last ninety days of your job are just as important as the first ninety days. Says Blount, "Despite its importance, the truth is that many senior executives botch their exits, often because they don't control the timing." The antidote to a botched exit is, according to Blount, "leaving well," which includes coaching "the team on performance right up to the end, while setting their successor up for success."[21]

If you've ever been unceremoniously dismissed from a job, or you know someone who has, that is an indication that you drove too far and missed your exit. And how does this happen? It happens when you've muted your GPS, which was trying to tell you to prepare for your exit. It happens when you're on autopilot or cruise control, not paying attention to what's going on down the road. There could be a wreck ahead or a traffic jam. You might even be asleep at the wheel. Before you know it, you've missed your exit and will need to make a U-turn and try to get back on track. Or worse, you might miss your exit and get caught up in a crash that will take you much time and care to recover from.

Life is short, and you owe it to yourself to ask these questions. You don't have time to waste. Every day is a gift. Why spend even one day off purpose?

Asking for Help

One thing to consider about rechecking your alignment is that you don't have to carry the burden all by yourself. In fact, it can be extremely beneficial to get others involved. This is where mentors and coaches, coworkers and colleagues, spouses and life partners, and others who have your best interest at heart come into play.

While the people who help you gain perspective should know you well, they should also be willing to be completely frank and honest with you—to hold no punches. They should also be able to take the fifty-thousand-foot view of your life and tell you what they see, for example: "I've tracked the narrative arc of your life for years now, and I've lately been hearing a degree of dissatisfaction and joylessness in your voice. I think it might be time for you to reconsider the career you're in and think about leaving for something that better suits you now."

Maybe you've been in the wrong job all along, or perhaps the job or you have changed and your work and your purpose are no longer aligned. Or maybe you've accomplished exactly what your Maker planned for you to accomplish and He has other plans for you. Whatever the reason, when it's time to go, you should go.

Besides friends and family and coworkers and colleagues, there's someone else you should be sure to consult: God. Prayer is a powerful tool for asking your Maker for direction and receiving advice from Him. I personally know numerous CEOs and other executives who take themselves out of their busy, day-to-day activities for a period of time to engage in silent retreats at which they have the opportunity to disconnect from the demands of the workplace, unplug from their smartphones and social media, and simply listen for God's voice—some for weeks at a time. It's remarkable how clearly you can hear God's voice when you slow down, reflect, and listen for Him.

A lot of people view this as a privilege, and they are right. It *is* a real gift to be able to leave the mundane cares of the world behind to listen for God's voice. Whether you're able to unplug for weeks at a time, hours at a time, or even just minutes at a time, listening clearly for the voice of your vocation is a necessity if you are going to receive your calling—what it is you are meant to do with your life. Not all of us will be able to go on a silent retreat and completely detach ourselves from our families and our everyday lives, but all of us have the opportunity to still our minds in a quiet place to hear God speak to our hearts.

As I mentioned earlier in this chapter, Sally Blount—former dean of the Kellogg School of Management—made the decision to step down from her position as dean after engaging in a silent retreat in July 2017. According to Blount, she has gone on silent retreats at least once a year for the past decade. While some of these retreats are fairly short—just two or three days—others are significantly longer, up to two weeks spent in silent contemplation. Blount says that she has learned three important leadership lessons as a result of her retreats: how to let go of connection, how to balance input with reflection, and how to build "leadership muscle."[22]

Let's explore each of these in turn:

LETTING GO OF CONNECTION. Although, says Blount, being completely alone with your thoughts while letting go of your dependence on virtual and social attachments can be difficult and even unsettling, it becomes easier the more you do it. "Even more importantly," says Blount, "you start to feel and think in new ways."

BALANCING INPUT WITH REFLECTION. Says Blount, "While asking for input and ideas is essential to leadership, you gain even more insight when you reflect deeply on that input." According to Blount, transformational thinking requires that we step away from our day-to-day habits and status-quo thinking. Silent retreats invite us to disrupt these well-worn behavioral patterns, generating new solutions for old problems.

DEVELOPING "LEADERSHIP MUSCLE." Blount says that although the silent retreats in which she participates were at first purely spiritual in nature, the retreats she engages in now not only nourish her spirit but "also nourish [her] work life in important ways." Blount provides an example of a time when her senior team wasn't hitting its goals. She engaged in a silent retreat for a few days and had an epiphany that provided the solutions she was looking for, resulting in a dramatic improvement in the team's performance.[23]

When I think about vocational courage, it is very much about clarity, which requires stillness to hear, but it is also the personal commitment to do what you hear. You can't do what you hear if you're not listening. The fact that you're not listening or not hearing God's voice does not mean that God is not speaking to you or that He is not ready to speak to you. God is faithful and is always ready to speak into the life of a willing listener. You may be in a dead zone because you're moving too fast or because you're incorporating too many of the wrong voices into your decision-making.

Remember the question I asked earlier in this book: Who do you ask when you have a question about your car's intended design or functionality? You don't ask just anyone; you ask the car's manufacturer—the organization that employs the people in whose minds it was conceived.

The same thing is true of us. Our society moves so fast today that most people think they're too busy to pray. I would argue that we're actually too busy *not* to pray. Each of us has so much potential and purpose in us that we can't afford to not pray. We have to slow down in order to accelerate—and for many of us, that's a paradigm shift.

There is much interest today in what is known as *mindfulness,* which is a modern name for the ancient spiritual practice of silence and solitude in which one is able to focus one's attention on what they are experiencing in a given moment. Silence and solitude in fact comprise a valuable spiritual discipline, and it is a valid approach for quieting your mind and clearly discerning the voice within you. In my experience, mindfulness is an effective way to slow down and to be prayerful and reflective. If "mindfulness" is the label someone needs to be prayerful, then I'm all in favor of it.

Regardless of what you call it, remember that prayer is a two-way conversation with God. Pray for answers to your questions. Pray for guidance and wisdom as you approach and enter the crossroads of your life. Pray for others who are in the same place in their own lives that you are in, that they too will receive the guidance and wisdom they need to make the right decisions moving forward. And when you pray, open yourself up to God and listen to the answers that He provides to you.

You may not understand why you have been called, or why now. We can always wonder why, but the truth is that it will become clear along the journey. We can't wait for the answer to the question of why before we decide to respond to the call. It's not your job to question God's wisdom.

It's your job to say "Yes."

8

Helping Others Develop
Vocational Courage

*If you have an opportunity to help others or incite change, it
feels like a moral obligation to do so.*

—ELIZABETH CHAMBERS

While Sheryl Sandberg currently serves as COO of
Facebook, the ubiquitous social media giant with
an average of more than 1.47 billion daily active users
worldwide[1] and total revenues in excess of $40 billion a
year,[2] her career took many twists and turns before she
landed a job as Mark Zuckerberg's right-hand woman, responsible for the company's day-to-day operations. Today,
Sheryl Sandberg is widely considered to be one of the most
powerful women in business, ranking number five on
Fortune's 2017 list.[3]

But Sandberg's early life bore no resemblance at all to
the high-powered Silicon Valley executive that she is
today. Sheryl Sandberg graduated from Harvard in 1991

where she majored in economics. One of her economics professors there was Larry Summers, who became a mentor to Sandberg. In 1991, Summers left Harvard to take a position as vice president of development economics and chief economist at the World Bank, and he recruited Sandberg to join him there as a research assistant. In 1993, Sheryl Sandberg left the World Bank to return to Harvard for her MBA, which she received in 1995. After graduation, Sandberg accepted a position at the global management consulting firm McKinsey & Company.

In 1995, Larry Summers was named deputy secretary of the US Treasury in the Clinton administration, and in 1996, Sheryl Sandberg accepted Summers's invitation to work for him there as his chief of staff. She stayed on at the US Department of the Treasury until Republican George W. Bush was elected the forty-third president of the United States in November 2000, and Summers and the rest of the Clinton administration were dismissed from the White House on Inauguration Day in January 2001.

Without a job, Sandberg reached out to Eric Schmidt, who was then CEO of Google—presenting him with a variety of career options she was considering at the time. His advice was direct and adamant: "No, no! Get out of the weeds. Go where there's fast growth, because fast growth creates all opportunities."[4] It turned out that the land of fast growth just happened to be Silicon Valley, in tech companies like Google. Ultimately, in 2001, Schmidt offered Sandberg the position as Google's vice president of global online sales and operations. She grew her team from just four people to thousands and is widely credited with turning Google's online advertising operation into a global—and highly profitable—powerhouse.

For many individuals this would be a great end to the story—the highly successful executive living happily ever after, with a lucrative portfolio of stock options in his or her pocket. But in many ways, Sheryl Sandberg was just getting started.

At a 2007 Christmas party thrown by former Yahoo COO Dan Rosensweig, Sandberg met Facebook founder Mark Zuckerberg. At the time, Facebook—founded in 2004—was struggling. While the company's base of active users and its costs were growing at a rapid pace, its profit was not. What Zuckerberg needed was someone who could take the reins of the company and lead it to profitability. He found that person in Sandberg.

Says Zuckerberg about his initial meeting with Sandberg at the Christmas party:

> *I'd almost given up on finding a person who'd be good in the COO role. But it was immediately clear from the crispness of her answers and the intensity she had when she talked that she was the kind of person who could do this.*[5]

According to Sandberg, during that first conversation, they asked each other deep questions related to their values: "What do you believe? What do you care about? What's the mission? It was very philosophical."[6]

Zuckerberg hired Sandberg as Facebook's COO in March 2008, and the rest is, as they say, history. Applying the lessons that she learned in her years at Google, Sandberg changed Facebook's online advertising model, and in September 2009—about a year and a half after Sheryl Sandberg accepted Zuckerberg's offer of employment—Facebook experienced a cash-flow-positive quarter for the very first time. Net income for 2017 was $15.9 billion.[7]

Clearly, Sheryl Sandberg has found what she was meant to do, but she didn't find her ultimate destination all by herself. Mentors played a key role in Sheryl Sandberg's career choices and pivots, opening her mind—and sometimes doors—to other possibilities. Ultimately, of course, Sandberg decided for herself which path to take. But instead of closing the door to potential career opportunities as they presented themselves, she carefully weighed each one against her own values and personal goals and then switched course—sometimes radically—when it made sense for her to do so.

If you are a leader, whether in your organization, in your community, or even in your family—one who has the opportunity to influence others—then I implore you to not be selfish. Don't be a brightly shining light living a vocationally courageous life and then just let others around you stay in the dark. By modeling vocational courage, you can awaken others to do the same, in much the same way that Sheryl Sandberg's mentors awakened vocational courage within her.

It's about setting an example, being a mentor/coach, and about being willing to invest in the growth of those around you. And you can ask questions such as, "Are you making the best and highest use of your time and talent every day? Are you fulfilling your own destiny? Are you in the right organization? Are you in the right role? Are you pursuing your vocation?" Recognize that you can't do the heavy lifting of pointing someone else in the direction of the vocation by yourself, but you can do something to help them along the path. In this chapter, we'll take a closer look at the power of helping others gain vocational courage.

In Service to Others

Noted humanitarian and MacArthur Foundation Fellowship grantee Marian Wright Edelman once wrote, "[S]ervice is the rent we pay for living. It is the very purpose of life and not something you do in your spare time."[8] As I consider her words, I fully understand that to be of service to other people—to lift as you climb—is part and parcel of one's vocation. Part of your legacy is not just what you accomplished in your short life, but how well positioned others beyond you were to carry out the work you started. It is often said for leaders that your success is linked to the success of your successor.

In chapter 3, I wrote about the doctoral advisor who helped guide me as I grappled with how obtaining a PhD and becoming a professor could detract from my calling as a pastor. She mentored me through that difficult time, essentially telling me not to overthink it and to do what I knew I was created to do. As I look back, I realize that she coached me to not only see the best in myself but also to achieve my best and highest purpose regardless of the obstacles that appeared to stand in my way. My advisor helped open my eyes to a world that I didn't even recognize existed. She encouraged me to build something that neither of us had quite seen built before. She pushed me. She coached me to pursue the path I was meant to walk.

Part of helping others have vocational courage is preparing them to do the work. If you're a leader, giving your people opportunities to learn new things, take on new duties, and advance in the organization and in their chosen fields is critical for their development. But there's also a flip side of that coin in terms of helping others to develop vocational courage. And that is knowing when you have a really talented person on your team who's doing amazing work but is in the wrong place; their growth is being stunted and their development is being arrested, but you don't want to let them go because you want them to be productive on your behalf. Sometimes helping others to develop vocational courage requires a fair amount of courage on the leader's part. Refusing to hold back talented people who have outgrown their current environment is an amazingly un-selfish way to help others develop vocational courage.

It takes courage for a manager to say, "Listen, I know we have a big project coming up in the next ninety days, but I see you're dying here. You need to be in a place that makes you feel alive and that puts your skills and talents and interests to better use. You have outgrown this organization and you have outgrown this role. I will do whatever I can to help you get where you belong, even if that means losing you."

Another approach to helping others develop vocational courage is to try to help your employee bring his or her purpose to work in a much more explicit way. You might say, "You're a gifted equity trader, and I really appreciate what you do for us and our bottom line. But I know that you also have a strong desire to work on projects that give back to the community in a variety of ways. So perhaps you can find ways to make the work you want to do in the community part of your work for our firm. If something is priority number one in your heart, it should also be reflected in your daily work. I'm willing to work with you to figure out how we can do that."

Max De Pree was born in Zeeland, Michigan, in 1924, and his father, D. J. De Pree, founded the Herman Miller Company, a furniture maker, a year earlier, in 1923. The company nearly failed in the wake of the Great Depression, but after Herman Miller revamped its product offerings—abandoning its traditional product offerings in favor of modern products that appealed to the fast-changing tastes of American consumers—the company's future was assured. Max De Pree joined Herman Miller in 1947 and he became CEO in 1980, serving in the position through 1987 and on the company's board through 1995. De Pree is widely considered to be one of America's best managers. Sadly, he passed away in 2017.

Max De Pree didn't originally plan to join the family furniture business; instead, he thought he would become a physician. In fact, De Pree was an undergraduate pre-med student at Haverford College, and he was accepted to Temple University Medical School. However, a couple of weeks after he received his acceptance, the offer was canceled as World War II broke out. De Pree enlisted in the army, and after basic training he was sent to Europe to join in the fight.

In his book *Leadership Is an Art*, De Pree explains:

> *The first responsibility of a leader is to define reality. The last is to say thank you. In between the two, the leader must become a servant and debtor. . . . Try to think about a leader, in the words of the gospel writer Luke, as "one who serves."*[9]

De Pree was referring to Luke 22:27: "For who is greater, he who sits at the table, or he who serves? Is it not he who sits at the table? Yet I am among you as the One who serves."[10]

In an interview, De Pree explains his idea of servant leadership in greater detail:

> *I think a servant leader is a person who is very committed to giving all the people for whom he is accountable a chance to be successful. Everybody has a strength. A lot of us have some weaknesses. I think a good leader spots strengths and builds on them and gives people a chance to be who they can be. Now, in order to do that, you have to know people. You have to take the time to get to know them. You see, good leaders only succeed really through the work of other people.*[11]

Max De Pree considers *Leadership Is an Art* to be an elaboration of the idea of leadership as a covenant between employer and employee. In an interview, he explains the difference between a covenantal and contractual model of leadership. The contractual approach is more transactional, focused on rules and regulations, performance metrics and targets, and the details of how unsatisfactory performance will lead to losing one's job. On the other hand, in a covenantal relationship, the leader makes a commitment to the employee and invites the employee to do the same in return. In the covenantal approach, neither party is looking for a reason to escape the relationship, but rather each seeks to go above and beyond to make

the relationship thrive, which ultimately makes high performance much more likely than a transactional, contractual relationship.

Max De Pree believed that employees bring certain
gifts to the workplace along with them, and God has en-
trusted these men and women to the care of their leaders.
In an interview with Peter Drucker, which appeared in
Drucker's book *Managing the Nonprofit Organization:
Principles and Practices,* De Pree explained:

> *I would have to begin with a very personal observa-
> tion, which is that I believe, first of all, that each of us
> is made in the image of God. That we come to life
> with a tremendous diversity of gifts. I think from
> there, a leader needs to see himself in a position of
> indebtedness. Leaders are given the gift of leadership
> by those who choose or agree to follow.*[12]

The best leaders care about their people. They don't
just view employees as cogs in a wheel, but as people who
have purpose, hopes, dreams, and vision. It is the rare leader
who is able to subordinate his or her own immediate exi-
gencies to do what's best, not just for the organization in
the near term, but also what's best for individuals in the
long term. The organization's interests and its people's interests do not have to be diametrically opposed or antithetical to one another.

In the contemporary marketplace, people have many options for where they can take their gifts and how they will express them in their daily work. Workers have more mobility between geographies, industries, and even companies within the same industry. People have a greater degree of choice about the trajectory of their careers at every stage, perhaps in a different way than people a generation ago, who, once they had selected a professional field, generally stayed put. Opportunity abounds, so it's up to leaders to provide employees with opportunities to use these gifts fully and meaningfully. It's up to leaders to provide their people the opportunity to link their purpose with the purpose and work of the organization.

Leaders have not just the opportunity but the duty to help those who work for and with them—whether by serving as connectors in employees' networks, or as mirrors for them to see when it's time to shift, or as people who help their employees work through the transitions in their careers and lives to navigate to the next level. Leaders have been entrusted with a great responsibility: stewarding the careers of the people who work for them. Because of this, they are in debt to their people. As Peter Drucker summarized at the end of his interview with Max De Pree, "And what they owe is really to enable people to realize their potential, to realize their purpose in serving the organization."[13]

What You Can Do

Unfortunately, many managers do not pay attention to the needs of their people, because they are themselves stretched and stressed. They often pay more attention to their own outcomes and their own goals than to their people. As I discussed in chapter 1, employee disengagement is rampant in most organizations across the United States and around the world. In many cases, disengagement is a classic sign that someone is off-purpose and that he or she is no longer aligned with the work. Leaders can detect that this is the case by paying attention to people's hopes and dreams and aspirations. This requires listening to people and getting to know them as human beings.

Ask, "What are your goals? What are your hopes? What are your aspirations? What are you trying to accomplish—not just in this organization, but with your life?" And ask, "Is this organization helping or hindering you?"

Another great way to help others develop vocational courage is to bake what I call *purpose screening* into the interview process. When you recruit and hire for an open position, it's tempting to hire someone who has the right skill set on paper, but who is not aligned with the organization's purpose. You should make every effort to avoid this temptation. Not offering someone a job is an act that can help a candidate develop vocational courage. You might tell the person, "Sharon, you look great on paper, but in my conversation with you it has become abundantly clear to me that you're made for more than this role. While we would love to have you be a part of our team here, bringing you onboard at this time—in this organization, in this role—would be doing you a grave disservice."

Even though you're under tremendous pressure to fill the position in the next ten days, and you've got someone who's amazingly qualified in front of you—ready to accept your offer—you know in your heart of hearts that the job is not right for that person. Great leaders recognize when this is the case and they guide the candidate to a more suitable position. You could say, "I can see that you've got purpose in you. I'm not saying 'no' because you are not qualified. I'm saying 'no' because you would be doing yourself a disservice by taking this job. I am happy to recommend you somewhere else."

Some companies are better than others when it comes to doing a good job of hiring people who fit their values. Southwest Airlines and Zappos are particularly good at it. In an interview, Zappos CEO Tony Hsieh explained:

> We've actually passed on a lot of really smart, talented people that we know can make an immediate impact on our top or bottom line, but if they're not good for the company culture, we won't hire them for that reason alone.[14]

The company has a variety of techniques for finding out whether or not a job candidate is going to be a good fit for the Zappos culture. During the interview process, for example, candidates are often requested to attend a department or company event so that they can meet the people with whom they will work—and those people can meet the candidates. This provides a vital source of input into the hiring decision.

Another technique checks to see how well candidates treat others. Says Tony Hsieh:

A lot of our candidates are from out of town, and we'll pick them up from the airport in a Zappos shuttle, give them a tour, and then they'll spend the rest of the day interviewing. At the end of the day of interviews, the recruiter will circle back to the shuttle driver and ask how he or she was treated. It doesn't matter how well the day of interviews went, if our shuttle driver wasn't treated well, then we won't hire that person.

And what if a job candidate is hired but he or she turns out not to fit into Zappos's unique culture? The company offers new hires three thousand dollars to quit the company. Apparently, the company does a pretty good job finding candidates who fit because, according to Hsieh, 97 percent of new employees turn down the offer. The offer provides misfits with an off-ramp, whether it is financial or otherwise. Even the most robust hiring practices are bound to make mistakes, because we're human, and people change.

Carmita Semaan, the founder of the previously mentioned Surge Institute, routinely faces this challenge. She started her organization in 2014 in Chicago, has already expanded to Oakland, California, and Kansas City, Missouri, and has plans for even further growth.

As Carmita grows and scales the organization, the temptation has been to find people who have the right skill set to do the work capably but may not be such a good fit with Surge Institute's mission. So she has deliberately grown the organization more slowly than some of her funders have asked her to grow it—not because there's a lack of demand, but because she wanted to provide adequate care and thoughtfulness to hiring the right people who were the right fit from a purpose perspective, not just from their skills.

Carmita's careful approach has served the organization well—ensuring that new hires are fully aligned with its mission, and as a result, that they closely link their own purposes with the purpose of Surge Institute. And it serves candidates and new hires well, providing them the opportunity to summon the vocational courage they need to be effective in their own careers and lives.

The Most Effective Approaches

Helping someone develop vocational courage requires having a good relationship with him or her *first* because it requires a degree of vulnerability and trust that you cannot easily reach absent the relational credibility. There's an element of "I'm trusting you with my future," and you can't have that conversation unless you're willing to be vulnerable. You're not going to be vulnerable with someone whom you don't trust, and we tend not to trust people very deeply if we don't have some type of relationship with that person at the start.

For these conversations, I've often found a coaching style is best, not a prescriptive one. One of the best things leaders can do to help others grow their vocational courage is to develop a coaching approach to leadership. The idea is to view the very act of leadership as being coaching intensive. Many people have been taught that good leadership is best achieved by being the smartest person in the room, having all the answers, and issuing directives. I disagree. I believe that some of the most effective leaders are not the ones who have all of the answers, but the ones who know how to ask the right questions in the right way at the right time. This is the heart of coaching, and this is what it takes to help people reach their own *aha* moments regarding vocational courage.

You have to be a good listener and you have to be honest about suspending your own agenda with people you are coaching, because, frankly, you're not the one who's doing the calling. You're just trying to help them discern the voice of the Caller and to develop the vocational courage they need to follow the direction they receive. You don't want your voice to be part of the problem; you just want to point them toward finding their own solution. Your job is to help them develop the courage and the commitment to do what they hear—not to be the one who's telling them what they are supposed to hear.

Parents often have a really hard time with this because they don't want their children to make the same mistakes they made growing up. So they end up pushing their children into activities and decisions that aren't necessarily the best fit for them. Recall the story in chapter 4 of successful entrepreneur Sabrina Kay, whose mother forced her into near-constant piano lessons in hopes of turning Sabrina into a world-class pianist. Kay grew to hate the piano and all it stood for, and she ultimately rejected it. The vocational courage she displayed led her directly to the one thing she was meant to do—and to tremendous success.

In some facets of life, a highly directive parental approach is absolutely the right thing to do, because some kids don't know what they don't know. But when it comes to figuring out what you're to do with your life, parents can be helpful in providing social and emotional support and in providing techniques for how to pray, meditate, listen, and hear. However, being the voice that is doing all the talking—prescribing exactly what their children can or cannot do—is often harmful.

Sometimes, it is a parent's or a loved one's voice that awakens our world to something that we did not know. This is not to suggest that parents need to just keep their advice to themselves. I have certainly benefited from the timely advice of my parents in many areas of my life. However, there is a careful balancing act between trying to live your life and aspirations through your child and really trying to orient your child for his or her best life—following the path laid out by God.

Kim Scott is a former CEO coach at Dropbox and Twitter, a member of the faculty at Apple University, and head of Doubleclick Online Sales and Operations at Google. She has had many other twists and turns in her career as she aligned—and realigned—with her purpose, including being the cofounder and CEO of a Silicon Valley start-up, working as a senior policy advisor at the Federal Communications Commission, managing a pediatric clinic in Kosovo, and starting up a Moscow-based diamond-cutting factory.

In her book *Radical Candor,* Scott explains that one of the most important things effective bosses do is to establish a trusting relationship with each one of the people who report to them. Says Scott in her book,

> *[T]hese relationships are core to your job. They determine whether you can fulfill your three responsibilities as a manager: 1) to create a culture of guidance (praise and criticism) that will keep everyone moving in the right direction; 2) to understand what motivates each person on your team well enough to avoid burnout or boredom and keep the team cohesive; and 3) to drive results collaboratively.*[15]

According to Scott, there are two dimensions that will help build trusting relationships between bosses and the men and women who work for them: care personally and challenge directly.

To *care personally* is to deeply care about the people who work for you, to share more than just your work self on the job, and to encourage your direct reports to follow your example. As Scott says in her book:

> *It's not enough to care only about people's ability to perform a job. To have a good relationship, you have to be your whole self and care about each of the people who work for you as a human being. It's not just business; it is personal, and deeply personal.*[16]

To *challenge directly* is to be frank and honest about people's performance—to let them know when their work is not good enough (and also when it *is* good enough) and set the bar high. Says Scott:

> *Delivering hard feedback, making hard calls about who does what on a team, and holding a high bar for results—isn't that obviously the job of any manager? But most people struggle doing these things.*[17]

She goes on to suggest that when you challenge your people, you're showing them you care personally about them. Both personal care and direct challenge are necessary and combine to yield what Scott calls *radical candor*.

In an onstage discussion with Kara Swisher for *Recode Decode*, Kim Scott tells about her own experience with radical candor when she worked for Sheryl Sandberg at Google. She had just made a presentation to Google cofounder Sergey Brin and the then CEO Eric Schmidt about the company's AdSense business. Scott was convinced the presentation went great—Google's online advertising venture was wildly successful, after all—until she walked out of the conference room and was immediately met by her boss, Sheryl Sandberg.

Sheryl said, "Why don't you walk back to my office with me?" She went on to tell Kim that she could benefit from a speech coach to correct some of the behaviors that were undermining her credibility. Although that constructive criticism was a tough pill to swallow and a hit to her ego, Scott recognized that it was also an expression of profound kindness, because nobody else cared enough about her over the course of her career to give her that feedback. Scott went on to praise Sandberg for having her people's best interests at heart, even when it might hurt their feelings, saying that Sandberg "didn't let her concern for our short-term feelings get in the way of saying what she needed to say for our long-term success."[18]

When you provide candid feedback and advice to others, you care for them personally and challenge them directly.

In this way, you'll build the strong relationships and trust required for you—and those to whom you are providing input—to be as effective as possible. It's these trusting relationships, typified by the capacity to have difficult conversations, that grant leaders permission to help others around them to develop their own vocational courage.

The Role of Following Up

Periodic follow-up can also be very beneficial to the process of helping others develop vocational courage, if they will allow it. Sometimes these are one-off conversations, and you don't have the opportunity to see the fruit of what the conversation produced. Sometimes you may only have one opportunity to have a single conversation with someone, and that one conversation could change his or her life, but you may never see that person again.

I experience this often as a professor, conference speaker, and pastor. I may preach a message one Sunday or give a keynote at a conference or facilitate a workshop with a group of executives visiting the campus, and if I never see the individuals again, I will have only had that one opportunity to influence their lives in a meaningful way. All I get is one shot—maybe twenty-five or thirty minutes, maybe ninety. But the fact remains that I may never see or hear from them again. They may never write or call or send an email, but their lives may have been positively impacted. So I look at each interaction as a high-stakes interaction—one that could significantly alter someone's life.

Every single human interaction has that life-changing, destiny-shaping potential, and the people you communicate with could be one interaction away from discovering why they were put on the planet. The conversations they have with you could be the very ones they needed, and your whole reason for being their manager, mentor, or coach could have been so that you were able to build up the relational equity with them to have this hard conversation that positioned them to live the life they were always meant to live.

I have found myself in situations where I have built relationships with people and we have one conversation, and then, all of a sudden, it becomes clear. The entire reason that I met these people and was able to build a relationship with them was so that we could have one life-altering conversation that will have incalculable ripple effects throughout history.

9

Vocational Courage
for Organizations

Whatever you do, you need courage. Whatever course you decide upon, there is always someone to tell you that you are wrong.

—RALPH WALDO EMERSON

The title of a *Wired* magazine article published on April 12, 2000, said it all: "Ben & Jerry's Sells Out."[1] The sellout the *Wired* article referred to was the decision by founders Ben Cohen and Jerry Greenfield to sell their deeply socially conscious business to a mammoth multinational consumer-products company, Unilever, headquartered in Rotterdam, Netherlands, for the princely sum of $326 million.

There was understandable concern among many observers that Unilever would push aside Ben & Jerry's social consciousness in favor of bottom-line results. As Cohen and Greenfield said in a statement at the time:

While we and others certainly would have pursued
our mission as an independent enterprise, we hope
that, as a part of Unilever, Ben & Jerry's will continue
to expand its role in society.[2]

Ice cream manufacturer Ben & Jerry's Homemade was
founded by hippie ice cream moguls Cohen and Greenfield in 1978 in a renovated Burlington, Vermont, gas sta-
tion, which they shared with a local farmer. Looking for a
start-up business opportunity, the pair first considered
opening a bagel shop; however, they deemed the required
equipment too expensive for their limited budget. Instead,
they purchased a five-gallon, rock-and-salt ice cream ma-
chine, took a $5.00 Penn State University correspondence
course in how to make ice cream (split two ways, with Ben
and Jerry each contributing $2.50 toward the total price),
and together soon started churning out their unique take
on this very traditional product, which eventually included
classic flavors such as Chunky Monkey, Half Baked, and
Cherry Garcia, along with the company's very first flavor,
Vanilla.[3]

Today, Ben & Jerry's is a household name, with estimated
annual revenues of $477 million.[4] But neither Cohen nor
Greenfield had a grand plan for the business that eventually became one of the nation's top-selling brands of ice
cream. Before the pair founded Ben & Jerry's, each was trying to figure out what they were uniquely put on the earth
to do.

Says Cohen:

I had dropped out of college and was trying to become a potter, but nobody wanted to buy my pottery, and Jerry had finished college and was trying to go to medical school, but nobody would let him into their medical school. So, I was delivering pottery wheels and working as a taxi driver, and he was a lab technician, working on rat brains and cow livers in a research lab, and neither of us really liked what we were doing with our lives. So we decided to try to start something together.[5]

In their case, the pain of rejection provided meaningful direction. Rejection provided redirection.

As it turned out, Ben and Jerry were uniquely put on this earth to make ice cream as a means of changing the world. To start up their business, Ben and Jerry each had to come up with an investment of four thousand dollars (Ben could only come up with two thousand, so his father contributed an additional two thousand), and a local bank kicked in a loan for four thousand dollars more.[6] As the company grew, the founders realized that they could use the business to advocate for social causes they supported. Says Jerry:

[W]e knew that's what would separate Ben & Jerry's— even more than the great flavors, it was important for

us to make our social mission a central part of the company.[7]

But Cohen and Greenfield knew that they still had to run a business. So they created a unique, three-part mission statement for Ben & Jerry's, with each part considered to be equally important: product excellence ("make fantastic ice cream"), economic performance ("sustainable financial growth"), and social impact ("make the world a better place").[8] Over time, the company's social mission encompassed such things as adopting chlorine-free packaging for its products (and thus not contributing to toxins released into the environment by the bleaching process), paying employees a living wage, pushing for political campaign finance reform, raising awareness about climate change, and becoming a B Corporation—committing itself to setting and achieving high social and environmental standards—and much more.

While the acquisition of Ben & Jerry's by Unilever could very well have damaged or even destroyed the social consciousness that the founders built into its DNA, for the most part, making the world a better place still plays a vital role for the company's current owners. At least part of the credit for this turn of events must surely go to a concession Cohen and Greenfield demanded during the acquisition negotiations with Unilever. To complete the acquisition, Unilever agreed to create an independent board of directors not under its control that would exist "in perpetuity."

As the Ben & Jerry's website points out, "It's not a governing body in a conventional sense," but this board is a powerful mechanism for ensuring that the vocational courage of Ben & Jerry's stays strong as it encourages (and sometimes pushes) the company to stay true to its progressive social activist roots.

The board currently numbers ten members, many of whom have been associated with Ben & Jerry's in one way or another for years—and three who were on the board of directors before the acquisition of the company by Unilever. According to Jennifer Henderson, CEO of Strategic Decisions, LLC, and a member of the Ben & Jerry's board since 1996, she and the other members have a measurable impact on the company's decision-making process. Says Henderson:

> We have the informal responsibility for sharing the genesis, background and history of the company with new board members and Unilever. This knowledge has been very important in setting the context for decisions the company makes today.[9]

With the help and guidance of its independent board of directors, Ben & Jerry's is well positioned to have the vocational courage necessary to, in the words of Jennifer Henderson, "continue to challenge, reinvent itself, and contribute to a just and caring world."[10] And, as Ben Cohen and Jerry Greenfield hoped when they sold their company to Unilever back in 2000, Ben & Jerry's is poised to continue expanding its role as a corporate force doing good in local communities and in the broader society.

All of the questions we ask of ourselves and other individuals can also be asked of organizations. Questions like: "What is our purpose? Who are we? What are we here for? What is success for us? Are we good citizens? Are we doing it ethically?" Many organizations—even nonprofits—can easily follow the allure of "success" to become what they're not designed to be.

In the case of nonprofits, there are huge issues around "mission creep"—taking on new responsibilities that have little or nothing to do with the organization's mission. An organization's leader might say, "We started an after-school program for kids in the community because we saw a need and next thing you know, we were also running a food pantry and homeless shelter." We rationalize, because we need money to pay our salaries and other costs, that it is fine to undertake activities that do not fit with the core of who we are. In the same way that individuals must practice vocational courage if they are to find lasting success, so must organizations.

What Is Vocational Courage in an Organizational Context?

Vocational courage in an organizational context is having clarity about what that organization's unique purpose is and making the difficult strategic decisions that are necessary to ensure that the organization's activities and strategies continue to align with that purpose. The organization fails to be itself when it acts in ways that are not consistent with its purpose, and if the purpose has strayed, then the organization is essentially losing itself.

As I survey today's business landscape, it has become clear to me that many organizations—primarily for-profit companies—are operating without a clear sense of purpose. In fact, I recently met with a group of top partners in a large law firm. When I asked these partners the question "What is your organization's purpose, and why do you exist?" not a single one had an answer. Not a single one!

This is disheartening, though unfortunately not surprising to me for several reasons. First, every organization needs to have a clear purpose that is more than just "making money" or "maximizing shareholder value." I've never met anyone who told me that what wakes them up in the morning is being able to make money for somebody else and keep a small slice of it to take home. Second, an inspiring purpose can be a powerful motivator for current employees—engaging them more strongly in their work and providing them with a reason to give the very best of themselves. Third, a company's purpose can be a strong magnet for attracting top talent—people who care about the same things the business cares about.

How is it, then, that an organization's executives—such

as the partners in the law firm I recently met with—or other employees do not know the purpose of the company to which they have devoted so much of their lives and time? How does that happen?

In the context of the law firm I visited, I suspect that many of the firm's lawyers were originally recruited into the firm without any sense of what its purpose was, beyond a general sense of making money while doing something productive. In my experience, such a result is not just a firm-level issue, but it is also an industry-level issue. A lot of people are attracted to BigLaw—the nation's largest law firms, with starting salaries of $160,000 and up[11]—because it's so financially lucrative. But many people are simply not bothering to talk about purpose, which sometimes opens the door to self-interested behavior—if not unethical or outright criminal behavior.

Increasingly, however, as these firms have to reach out to a younger workforce to recruit talent, they're finding that many millennials insist upon this confluence of purpose and profit, merging their work and their impact. As a result, the firms are just beginning to wrestle with how they can infuse their work with purpose and meaning—or in many cases, distill and highlight the purpose and meaning already present in the work that simply goes unmentioned. Clearly, as I discovered when I asked the partners of that large law firm if they could explain their purpose, there's still a long way to go.

According to Deloitte's Millennial Survey 2017:

Being involved with "good causes" and not-for-profit organizations—whether directly or through opportunities provided by employers—helps millennials feel empowered and able to influence the world around them.[12]

Deloitte found that 77 percent of the millennials surveyed have personally participated in a "good cause" or nonprofit.

And the next generation in line after millennials—widely known as Generation Z—takes this focus on purpose a step further. In a survey of more than two thousand young people, the Lovell Corporation reported:

While Millennials seek jobs that provide stability, convenience, and balance, Generation Z is more readily concerned with fueling their passions and taking pride in the work they do. For the first time, we see a generation prioritizing purpose in their work.[13]

According to the survey, the top-five work value priorities for the members of Generation Z are: (1) Doing interesting work; (2) Working for an organization you're proud of; (3) Doing work you're passionate about; (4) Having the information you need to do your job; and (5) Continuous learning. As the Lovell Corporation report goes on to say, "We can describe Millennials as driven by growth and lifestyle, and Generation Z as driven by growth and passion."[14]

Connie Lindsey is executive vice president and head of corporate social responsibility and global diversity and inclusion for Northern Trust, a Chicago-based financial services firm. She often talks about people wanting "to connect their soul with their role." I believe that connecting your soul with your role is critically important for organizations as well, because no matter how skilled an organization may be at producing its products/services, its reason for being is more important than its key activities/products/services. An organization's *why* sits at the foundation of its culture, which is any organization's most precious resource and only source of sustainable competitive advantage. As soon as the organization's *why* changes, its *what* ought to change, too, and if employees aren't on board with these shifts, then the outcomes can be confusion, lower morale, and suboptimal performance.

Leaders show organizational vocational courage when they are able to confront and act on the fact that the organization is straying from its sense of purpose. This requires first ensuring the clarity of purpose, and then also making sure that the commitment to living out the purpose is strong.

It all comes down to an organization's culture, which has three important building blocks:

- Its purpose—the foundational reason it exists
- Its principles—no more than a handful of core values that align with the organization's purpose and express how the organization goes about its work
- Its practices—the organization's routines, policies, processes, and activities

So part of vocational courage for organizations is making sure that what we are doing is aligned with who we are, and not just going after things that sound cool or after strategic opportunities that seem potentially lucrative. If they are not aligned with who we are as an organization, or if they are going to cause us to somehow compromise our integrity, then we should say "No." It can take a tremendous amount of courage to say "No" to things that sound interesting but that are not what we should be doing based on why we say we exist and who we say we are. Every opportunity to grow or make money is not necessarily the right opportunity for a business.

You don't have to be a nonprofit or social benefit organization to have a clear sense of purpose. Some of today's most successful companies know very well why they exist. The Walt Disney Company strives to be "one of the world's leading producers and providers of entertainment and information."[15] Nike wants to "bring inspiration and innovation to every athlete in the world."[16] Walmart is motivated by this purpose: "[W]e save people money so they can live better."[17]

Every organization should have a clear sense of purpose, just as every individual should have a clear sense of purpose. Purpose is not *what* we do but *why* we exist. Maximizing shareholder value is a key performance indicator, but it is not why you exist as an organization. There are plenty of organizations that can create shareholder value, so existing solely to create shareholder value is neither necessary nor sufficient. Why your organization uniquely exists is a much different conversation, which has implications for how you attract and retain talent, based on that value proposition.

Why Some Organizations Lose Their Way

Some corporations become so enamored with maximizing shareholder value that losing their way is fairly easy. Executives—especially those in publicly traded companies— are naturally disincentivized to lead vocationally courageous organizations, because they are expected to lead, manage, and respond to the stock market in ninety-day increments, from one quarterly earnings call to the next quarterly earnings call.

Because they are incentivized to manage their public businesses in ninety-day increments (millions of dollars of their own stock options may depend on the quarterly results), executives are often dissuaded from thinking about the deeper question of whether or not something is the right thing for the organization to do for its long-term health and vitality. In many cases, shareholders (including senior executives whose compensation may include significant grants of stock) are incentivized to only care about what's going to make them money in the near- or mid-term, not benefit the organization over a period of decades.

The good news is that there are executives (I personally know many) who, when faced with a board and shareholders that want them to act in ways that are not vocationally courageous, will walk away instead of compromising the purpose and values of the organizations for which they work. They would rather resign than do something they don't believe in. This is vocational courage in action.

To avoid losing their way, an organization's leadership has to ask two sets of questions. First: "Why do we exist?" and "What really matters?" Second: "Are our day-to-day actions aligning with what we say matters and who we say we are?" These questions are easier to answer in start-ups, which often have their founders and a strong founding culture in place, but every organization had to start at some point, and those questions are crucial to ask and repeat at different stages in an organization's history.

For companies that have outlived their founders, it's particularly important that their purpose and values are hardwired into the corporate culture and can survive the whims of future executives who may care more about their bonuses than whether or not their businesses are living out their true purpose.

From the company's founding in 1976, Steve Jobs was the chief visionary for Apple Computer. In 1983, Jobs brought in John Sculley—then CEO of PepsiCo—to run Apple as its new CEO, enabling Jobs to focus his efforts on leading the team that would introduce the Macintosh computer. However, when the new computer was introduced to lukewarm sales—putting financial strain on Apple—the company's board removed him from his position at the head of the Macintosh group. He decided to leave the company, taking with him the burning-hot flame of purpose that made Apple different from every other computer manufacturer.

But Steve Jobs didn't give up his vision for what the future of computing could and should be. Said Jobs about this difficult time:

> *I even thought about running away from [Silicon] Valley. But something slowly began to dawn on me. I still loved what I did. The turn of events at Apple had not changed that one bit. And so I decided to start over.*

Starting over for Steve Jobs meant founding computer company NeXT in 1985 and computer-animated film company Pixar in 1986.

Over the next decade, Apple lost sight of its purpose, and its financial fortunes suffered: by 1997 the company was close to bankruptcy. It was then that Jobs and Apple reached an agreement to merge NeXT and Apple, and within a few months, Jobs returned to the helm of Apple as CEO. His return brought about an unprecedented period of innovation and growth with the release of a deluge of new products, including iPod, iPhone, iPad, iMac, iTunes, and many others.

Ridden with cancer, in 2011 Steve Jobs resigned from the company he founded, entrusting it to new CEO Tim Cook. In an email written to Apple's employees, Cook made it clear that Steve Jobs's founding vision and Apple's unique culture would be his ongoing central focus. Said Cook:

> *I want you to be confident that Apple is not going to change. I cherish and celebrate Apple's unique principles and values. Steve built a company and culture that is unlike any other in the world and we are going to stay true to that—it is in our DNA. We are going to continue to make the best products in the world that delight our customers and make our employees incredibly proud of what they do.*[18]

The story of Apple's decline after founder Steve Jobs left is less about Steve Jobs himself and more about an organization that had lost its soul and its purpose. The people who led Apple were no longer in touch with the qualities that made the company different from every other computer company in the world at the time—its unique reason for being. That is why it is particularly important to institutionalize and hardwire purpose and values into the organization's culture and DNA, as opposed to leaving them up to the presence of a particular personality.

Apple should not rise or fall on Steve Jobs or on people's memory of Steve Jobs. He's now a historical figure—he's not coming back—and fewer people at Apple personally knew and worked with him. Much the same thing happened with the civil rights movement. There are still people alive today who marched with Dr. King, who spent time with him and experienced his deep sense of purpose. As these men and women fade into eternity, the civil rights movement is further removed from the men and women who founded it and built its purpose, values, and culture. This is why having an organization that retains institutional memory is important.

I have seen this in churches where a pastor will retire or pass away, and a new pastor steps in to take his place. The people say, "This new pastor is destroying the essence of what has made us who we are down through the years," and they are resistant to his message and leadership. But what do we actually have of "who we were before" except for our anecdotal memories of the previous pastor's personality or teaching? Has any of this been institutionalized in the church's policies, procedures, and practices?

In many cases, the answer is no. If the church's purpose, principles, and traditional practices are not codified, institutionalized, and hardwired into the organization's routines, then when the pastor dies or leaves, it often disappears with him.

This is not to suggest that everyone always gets it right; vocational courage is not about perfection, especially when you think about it at the organizational level, where it's much harder to accomplish. It's hard enough for individuals to consistently be vocationally courageous with themselves, let alone to ensure that a diverse collection of individuals remains vocationally courageous. However, by recording and institutionalizing the things that make an organization uniquely what it is—along with hiring people who are aligned with the organization's purpose—businesses can also be vocationally courageous.

The Problem of Mission Creep in Nonprofits

Mission creep occurs with nonprofits when—faced with the need to acquire or develop more resources, usually in the form of grant funds or greater visibility—they violate their reason for being by taking on activities that are not part of the organization's purpose. For example, an organization that advocates for cancer research decides to open a shelter for battered women because some battered women in the area have cancer. By doing this, they are able to obtain a million-dollar grant from a foundation with the mission of helping to remove battered women from abusive homes. While their hearts are in the right place, they are potentially making a huge strategic mistake by expanding their purpose merely to capture the grant funding.

Another example is a nonprofit, community-based organization that works with inner-city kids in an after-school program. The program administrator notices that a lot of the kids enrolled in the program are hungry, so she decides to start a food pantry. As it turns out, some of the parents of these kids who have come to the after-school program are unemployed, so the nonprofit next creates a job training center. The nonprofit's suite of programs continues to mushroom in ways that are tangentially connected to the nonprofit's mission, but not at the core of it.

The activities the organization is undertaking are helping people live better lives. But as is also true with individuals and the career choices they make, just because you *can* do something doesn't mean you *should* do something. It may be good to do, but not good for *you* to do.

When Frances Hesselbein took over as CEO of the Girl Scouts of the USA in 1976, one of the first things she did to turn around an organization that had been in decline for a number of years was to open up membership to *all* girls, regardless of race or socioeconomic status. She ordered revisions to the Girl Scout handbook to include pictures of all kinds of girls. Said Hesselbein:

If I'm a Navajo child on a reservation, a newly ar-
rived Vietnamese [immigrant] child, or a young girl
in rural Appalachia, I have to be able to open [the
Girl Scout handbook] and find myself there.[19]

In 2015, someone made a donation to the Girl Scouts of
Western Washington. Not just any donation, but a check for
$100,000—about one-third of the organization's annual
budget. There was just one catch: the donor sent a letter that
read, "Please ensure that your gift will not be used to support transgender girls. If you can't, please return the money."
While the Girl Scouts national organization allows local councils to make the decision whether or not to include
transgender girls in the organization on a case-by-case
basis, Western Washington Council CEO Megan Ferland
immediately knew what to do. She mailed the check back
to the donor.

When news of Ferland's decision went public, she decided to start an Indiegogo campaign to make up for the lost
donation. Within three days, donations totaled more
than $250,000, and by the time the fund-raising campaign
drew to a close one month after it started, the Western
Washington Girl Scouts had raised more than $335,000.
Megan Ferland showed tremendous vocational courage on
behalf of her organization, demonstrating to her team, her
volunteers, her Girl Scouts, and her community that the
council would stay true to the purpose for which it was
created.

How Organizations Can Determine
What They Are Meant to Be

So what is the impact that your business is uniquely suited to create—in other words, why does it exist? What is the net impact of its existence on the world? For established organizations, I like to ask them the question, "If your company goes out of business tomorrow, what is the net impact on society or the marketplace?" Is the net impact purely an economic one? Or is there some broader impact, such as the loss or absence of something the organization was uniquely able to provide to the marketplace or to the community or to society that no other organization can? And if it's the latter, then that helps the organization understand what its unique purpose is in a very crowded marketplace—both on the for-profit and not-for-profit sides.

If some companies were to go out of business tomorrow, probably no one aside from the owner would care. Some companies, on the other hand, would have a disproportionately large impact if they were to go out of business tomorrow. *Many* people would care.

While toy store Toys"R"Us had already faded into a shadow of its former glory, having filed for bankruptcy protection in September 2017, when it was announced in March 2018 that the company would close or sell its remaining stores, many people were saddened by the news. Why? Because the store provided a unique experience for shoppers—a huge store dedicated to selling toys at a discount, an indoor field of dreams for millions of children who frequented its miles of aisles. Toys"R"Us was not just a toy store, it was a destination for generations of children.

Patagonia—the outdoor and adventure equipment and clothing retailer—is an example of a company that *many* would care about if it went out of business, mostly because its customers are closely tied to Patagonia's purpose. The company (then called Chouinard Equipment) was cofounded in 1965 by mountain climber Yvon Chouinard and aeronautical engineer and climber Tom Frost to produce and sell strong, light, simple, and functional climbing hardware— such things as pitons and aluminum chocks that climbers use to scale rock faces. In the 1970s, the company added clothing to its product line and renamed the company Patagonia. According to the company website, the name was chosen because:

> *To most people, especially then, Patagonia was a name like Timbuktu or Shangri-La, far-off, interesting, not quite on the map. Patagonia brings to mind, as we once wrote in a catalog introduction, "romantic visions of glaciers tumbling into fjords, jagged windswept peaks, gauchos and condors." It's been a good name for us, and it can be pronounced in every language.*[20]

Founder Yvon Chouinard has specifically built Patagonia to promote and support the environment, human rights, sustainability, and other social causes that he so deeply believes in. People who share these same values have become some of the company's most vocal and loyal customers. Says Chouinard:

> *As a company, we've made a contract with our customers to make clothing as responsibly as possible. That includes asking customers to think twice before they buy anything. Do you really need it, or do you just want it? If you really need it and buy from us, we promise to fix it, no matter what. I know it sounds crazy, but every time I have made a decision that is best for the planet, I have made money. Our customers know that—and they want to be part of that environmental commitment.*[21]

Patagonia has tremendous organizational vocational courage. The company and the people who run and work for it are clear on the purpose of the company, and they are fully aligned with it: they live and breathe it in all they do, making it stronger with each passing day. According to Patagonia's published reason for being:

> *For us at Patagonia, a love of wild and beautiful places demands participation in the fight to save them, and to help reverse the steep decline in the overall environmental health of our planet. We donate our time, services and at least 1% of our sales to hundreds of*

grassroots environmental groups all over the world
who work to help reverse the tide.[22]

All the questions we have been asking throughout this book for individuals are the exact same questions organizations should be asking themselves. By organizations, I mean key leaders who set the organization's agenda—both in terms of the organization's strategy and activities, but also in terms of who they're hiring and what they are trying to sell as a value proposition for working there.

Once they get the answers to these questions, this is where embedding comes in—hardwiring or institutionalizing these insights into the practices and routines and policies of the organization. By doing this, these things become part of the organization's soul, guiding decision-making and dictating actions.

During the course of this embedding process, people who aren't aligning with the purpose will either need to become aligned or move on. And these should be the criteria that the company uses to evaluate people who are recruited to join the organization. They also need to look at the organization's system of incentives and rewards. Does this system reinforce our purpose, values, and principles? Or are we rewarding behaviors that run counter to our purpose and our principles?

When people feel closely engaged and tightly aligned with the mission of the organization, and really feel a part of it, they are going to be much more courageous in the decisions they make, because the organization matters to them. Feeling this engagement and alignment with purpose requires working in the place you are meant to be, for an organization that has a purpose that resonates with you personally. An organization will have a very hard time getting this right if its leadership is not in the right place and in the right roles.

For people to know they are in the right place, the organization has to collectively know *it* is in the right place—the right market(s), the right communities, and operating with the right vocationally courageous strategy. It has to have a clear idea of what its purpose is, and its leadership team must support this purpose and ensure it is infused throughout everything the organization does and the decisions people make. In this way, the organization and the individuals who work for it can be vocationally courageous and bring the very best of themselves to their work, to their customers, and to the world.

The Contagion of Courage

History has shown us that courage can be contagious.

—MICHELLE OBAMA

As she prepared to conclude her speech to the graduating class of 2012 at the Northwestern University Kellogg School of Management, the Reverend Roslyn Brock, former chair of the National Association for the Advancement of Colored People (NAACP), exclaimed, "Courage must not skip this generation!"

Her words on the occasion of my doctoral convocation have reverberated through the corridors of my mind for years. I have wondered what it means for courage to skip a generation. I have wondered how I can do my part to make sure that it does not skip mine. I hope this book will prove to be a small contribution to that end.

The movie *The Help* sheds a little light on what it means for courage to not skip a generation. This film, adapted from a Kathryn Stockett novel of the same name, chronicles the story of two African American domestic workers in white households in the segregated and racially charged American South of the mid-twentieth century who dared to stand up and courageously share their stories of the pain and hatred they endured. By going against the prevailing ethos of racism and bigotry of the day, the young white writer who recorded these women's narratives put herself in the way of social—if not physical—backlash.

One scene depicts the writer's mother retrospectively reflecting upon her own life and lamenting to her daughter that "courage sometimes skips a generation." In other words, she was conveying the fact that she regretted not living as courageously as she could have, while at the same time she was applauding her daughter for the courage she was demonstrating in her life. Through the bold act of going against the status quo, the young writer demonstrated the courage necessary to make a difference.

When it comes to having the unflinching commitment to receive clarity regarding your life's work and demonstrating the wholehearted faithfulness to live it out as best you can through your daily work, we cannot afford for vocational courage to skip a generation. This is not about picking the most glamorous profession or the career trajectory with the highest prospects for wealth creation, or even taking up one's passion project. As my friend Connie Lindsey says, it's about connecting your "soul with your role." In short, it's all about purpose. And in a world where 83 percent of people rank their ability to find meaning in their daily work as one of their top three priorities in the workplace, the need for vocationally courageous leaders is especially urgent.[1] Believe it or not, your vocational courage can make a difference—and not just for your own quality of life.

You may think that your demonstration of vocational courage would have no impact on anybody else but you, but nothing could be further from the truth. While your own human flourishing is a worthy end unto itself, as Michelle Obama said, "[H]istory has shown us that courage can be contagious." Your demonstration of vocational courage may be the spark that catalyzes a scientific breakthrough or ignites a spiritual revival or transforms your community for good. Or in the case of my own life, seeing my parents and mentors demonstrate vocational courage inspires me to do the same every day.

You never know who you're influencing, but somebody is watching you—whether it is a friend, family member, colleague, or even someone from a distance. Those people may not know that you're aligning your daily work with your life's work, but they'll surely be able to see that you're burning brightly and walking with an uncommon grace, which they'll want to exemplify in their own life. Your vocational courage *will* be contagious. I bid you Godspeed on your journey to purpose.

Acknowledgments

First and foremost, I give glory to God for loving me and calling me into His service. The completion of this book is a testament to the grace of God upon my life. I am confident that without Christ, I would be nothing. In knowing the Lord, I have come to understand who I have been made to be, what I have been made to do, and why I have been made to do it. God is my Creator, my Caller, and the source of my courage to live into my vocation—and to complete this book.

I also hasten to express my most profound gratitude to my wife, partner, friend, and childhood sweetheart, Tammy, whose love and unwavering support have blessed my life. Partnering with her in life and purpose brings me indescribable joy. Her encouragement and sacrifice through the process of bringing this book to life are appreciated beyond words.

I thank my son, Nolan, now a child, whose life and future inspire this book. This book contains my hopes for him and every other person on the planet—that they will know the purpose for which they have been made and pursue its fulfillment every day of their lives.

Thanks also to my Mom and Dad for putting me on the right path from day one, unconditionally loving and supporting me, and for being such steadying influences through every season of my life. I have only grown in my deep appreciation for how they raised me since I have become a parent myself. Their love, guidance, encouragement, and modeling have made an indelible impact on my life, which words cannot adequately convey. Without the foundation they established for me, I would not have had the confidence to dare to dream big dreams, attempt the seemingly impossible, or write a book about aligning your daily work with your life's work.

Thanks also to Thomas A. Kochan, the George Maverick Bunker Professor of Management at the Massachusetts Institute of Technology's Sloan School of Management. Tom took a chance on me as a chemical engineering undergraduate who was trying to find his way by affording me the opportunity to work closely with him as a research associate. It was Tom's mentorship and guidance that opened the world of organizational behavior to me, which is a significant domain for the accomplishment of my life's work. Were it not for Tom, I would not have pursued my PhD or become a professor at one of the world's leading business schools. I would not have even conceived of occupying the platform to influence the practice of leadership and management in the global marketplace. I have great admiration for him, and the friendship that has resulted from our professor-student relationship has been a tremendous blessing. I am most grateful to Tom for his early guidance and sponsorship, which set me down the path that I am on.

I am also thankful for the person to whom Tom sent me to continue my academic training—Professor Katherine W. Phillips, the Reuben Mark Professor of Organizational Character at Columbia Business School (who was on the faculty of Northwestern University's Kellogg School of Management at the time). Kathy was my doctoral advisor at Northwestern, and without fear of equivocation, I can safely conclude that she is the best advisor in the history of the academy. Without question, I am better for the benefit of Kathy's time, her sound personal and professional advice, and her insightful scholarly guidance and feedback. It was her unselfish commitment to my development and vocational courage that gave me the confidence to dare to take the path that I am now on. Her timely advice helped me understand what vocational courage actually means. I cannot possibly thank her enough.

Thanks to the many audiences of hundreds of leaders around the world who received the idea of vocational courage so warmly and approached me after my speeches to ask me, "Do you have a book?—because I need your speech in a book." To know that this idea has literally changed lives and awakened dreams and visions that were once dormant is a tremendous privilege. It is in no small measure owing to their collective persistence in demanding that this book be written that it is now a reality.

And thanks to the people who supported me in this book project with editorial support, coaching and wise counsel, and research assistance along the way, including George Witte of St. Martin's Press, Peter Economy, Giles Anderson, and my self-proclaimed Kellogg VC Squad, a wonderful cadre of young graduate students at Northwestern University's Kellogg School of Management who heard me lecture about the idea of vocational courage and immediately latched on to it and committed themselves to providing their research assistance and feedback—Max Banaszak, Wit Chanyarungrojn, Jeff Hofer, Kevin Keenan, Ferrona Lie, Julia Lynch, Kaitlin Moore, Eleanor Sheers, Rob Shiffer, Adela Tomsejova, and Victoria Yang. Their passion, ideas, and feedback as the concept of vocational courage took greater shape were absolutely invaluable.

I must also express my gratitude to every leader I had the opportunity to work for, with, or watch along the way. From observing their lives and hearing their stories, I've learned about how important vocational courage is for leaders in every season of life. I've learned about how having vocational courage can accelerate impact and deep fulfillment and at the same time how not demonstrating it can tear apart families and careers. I thank them for giving me the privilege of a front-row seat to witness their lives up close and teaching me many valuable lessons—sometimes unintentionally.

Finally, I have dedicated this book to my childhood pastor, the legendary and sainted Bishop Arthur M. Brazier from the Apostolic Church of God in Chicago. Our relationship started as one between a pastor and parishioner, but over the years grew into a mentor-protégé relationship and cherished friendship. Though he passed away in 2010, he remains my model for stewarding a faithful ministry that can have far-reaching influence and impact in multiple spheres of society. He demonstrated the importance of listening carefully for the guiding voice of God and then faithfully living out the guidance you've received from God. Not a day goes by that I don't think of him or wish I could call him for advice, but I'm grateful for the time and wisdom he so generously shared.

Notes

1. What Is Success?

1. www.nytimes.com/1997/09/25/business/tug-of-home-is-stronger-than-the-pull-of-the-office.html
2. www.theatlantic.com/business/archive/2014/07/why-pepsico-ceo-indra-k-nooyi-cant-have-it-all/373750/
3. http://buzz.strayer.edu/latest-posts/success-means-americans/
4. www.gallup.com/businessjournal/195803/employees-really-know-expected.aspx?g_source=EMPLOYEE_ENGAGEMENT&g_medium=topic&g_campaign=tiles
5. https://hbr.org/2013/07/employee-engagement-does-more
6. https://hbr.org/2018/01/how-automation-will-change-work-purpose-and-meaning
7. www.oprah.com/spirit/how-oprah-winfrey-found-her-purpose

2. Who Am I?

1. https://en.oxforddictionaries.com/definition/consciousness
2. https://news.nationalgeographic.com/2015/08/150826-science-brain-mind-alzheimers-neuroscience-self-ngbooktalk/
3. https://factfinder.census.gov/faces/tableservices/jsf/pages/productview.xhtml?pid=PEP_2015_PEPASR6H&prodType=table

4. Barack Obama, *Dreams from My Father: A Story of Race and Inheritance* (New York: Broadway Books, 2004), 10.
5. Ibid., 302.
6. Ibid., 305.
7. Ibid., 376–377.
8. https://en.oxforddictionaries.com/definition/identity
9. www.biblestudytools.com/nkjv/romans/12.html

3. Why Am I Here?

1. Viktor Frankl, *Man's Search for Meaning* (Boston: Beacon Press, 2006, 83.
2. Ibid., 77.
3. Richard Dawkins, *The God Delusion* (New York: Mariner Books, 2006), 126.
4. www.shortercatechism.com/resources/wsc/wsc_001.html
5. www.pewresearch.org/fact-tank/2015/05/13/a-closer-look-at-americas-rapidly-growing-religious-nones/
6. www.utilitarian.net/bentham/
7. Parker Palmer, *Let Your Life Speak: Listening for the Voice* (San Francisco: Jossey-Bass, 1999), 36.

4. Am I Running the Right Race?

1. Gabriele Junkers, ed., *Is It Too Late?: Key Papers on Psychoanalysis and Ageing* (London: Karnac Books, 2006), 1–26.
2. "The U-Bend of Life," *The Economist*, December 16, 2010, also available at www.economist.com/node/17722567
3. www.goodreads.com/author/quotes/19982.Frederick_Buechner
4. www.calledthejourney.com/blog/2014/11/29/parker-palmer-on-calling-that-which-you-cant-not-do
5. www.yesmagazine.org/issues/working-for-life/now-i-become-myself
6. https://en.wikiquote.org/wiki/E._E._Cummings
7. http://sabrinakay.com/do-you-know-the-4-ingredients-to-career-success-and-life-happiness/
8. Ibid.
9. www.naacp.org/latest/courage-will-not-skip-this-generation-2/

5. Am I Running the Race Well?

1. www.navy.com/careers/navy-seal#ft-key-responsibilities
2. https://news.utexas.edu/2014/05/16/mcraven-urges-graduates-to
   -find-courage-to-change-the-world
3. https://about.hyatt.com/en.html

6. What's Courage Got to Do with It?

1. www.washingtonpost.com/news/on-small-business/wp/2017/10
   /19/study-71-percent-of-employees-are-looking-for-new-jobs/
   ?utm_term=.a09d5a9c1ae6
2. www.bls.gov/careeroutlook/2017/article/new-career.htm
3. http://home.uchicago.edu/~nklein/PerceivedChange.pdf
4. https://brenebrown.com
5. Ibid.
6. www.yesmagazine.org/issues/working-for-life/now-i-become
   -myself
7. https://nces.ed.gov/pubs2018/2018434.pdf
8. www.theatlantic.com/magazine/archive/2016/04/quit-your-job
   /471501/
9. Ibid.
10. Ibid.
11. http://edition.cnn.com/2008/WORLD/africa/06/24/mandela
    .quotes/
12. www.biblestudytools.com/nkjv/1-corinthians/9.html
13. www.biblestudytools.com/nkjv/jeremiah/20-9.html
14. www.biblestudytools.com/nkjv/exodus/4.html

7. Rechecking Your Alignment

1. www.chicagotribune.com/news/data/ct-michelle-obama-chicago
   -map-htmlstory.html
2. https://web.archive.org/web/20090116125432/http://style.com
   /vogue/feature/2007_Sept_Michelle_Obama
3. Ibid.
4. www.washingtonpost.com/wp-dyn/content/story/2008/10/03
   /ST2008100302144.html

5. https://womenintheworld.com/2015/04/14/an-inside-look-at -michelle-obamas-life-before-the-white-house/
6. https://ucsc.uchicago.edu/
7. www.whitehouse.gov/about-the-white-house/first-ladies/michelle -obama/
8. https://en.wikiquote.org/wiki/Michelle_Obama
9. www.sofi.com/blog/entrepreneurs-share-how-to-start-a-business -while-paying-down-student-loans/
10. John Wood, *Leaving Microsoft to Change the World: An Entrepreneur's Odyssey to Educate the World's Children* (New York: HarperBusiness, 2006), 6.
11. Ibid.
12. Ibid., 9
13. www.businesstimes.com.sg/magazines/wealth-april-2018/finding -purpose-in-room-to-read
14. www.roomtoread.org/impact-reach
15. http://www.centerforgiving.org/Portals/0/2006%20Cone%20Mil lennial%20Cause%20Study.pdf
16. www.forbes.com/sites/hecparis/2017/01/30/why-its-a-great-idea -to-change-career-when-you-are-40/
17. http://news.gallup.com/businessjournal/191459/millennials-job -hopping-generation.aspx
18. https://en.wiktionary.org/wiki/heuristics
19. https://news.northwestern.edu/stories/2017/september/sally -blount-to-step-down-as-kellogg-dean/
20. https://poetsandquants.com/2017/09/07/kellogg-dean-sally-blount -to-step-down/
21. www.forbes.com/sites/sallyblount/2018/02/12/leaving-well-why -the-last-90-days-matters-more-than-the-first-90/#ef7f8a76d7e9
22. www.linkedin.com/pulse/burnt-out-work-consider-silent-retreat -sally-blount/?trk=mp-reader-card
23. Ibid.

8. Helping Others Develop Vocational Courage

1. https://newsroom.fb.com/company-info/
2. https://s21.q4cdn.com/399680738/files/doc_financials/2017/Q4 /Q4-2017-Press-Release.pdf
3. http://fortune.com/most-powerful-women/

4. www.vogue.com/article/sheryl-sandberg-what-she-saw-at-the-revolution
5. Ibid.
6. www.newyorker.com/magazine/2011/07/11/a-womans-place-ken-auletta
7. https://s21.q4cdn.com/399680738/files/doc_financials/2017/Q4/Q4-2017-Press-Release.pdf
8. Marian Wright Edelman, *The Measure of Our Success: A Letter to My Children and Yours* (Boston: Beacon Press, 1992), 6.
9. Max De Pree, *Leadership Is an Art* (New York: Crown Business, 2004), 11–12.
10. www.biblestudytools.com/nkjv/luke/22-27.html
11. https://tobiascenter.iu.edu/research/oral-history/audio-transcripts/de-pree-max.html
12. Peter Drucker, *Managing the Nonprofit Organization: Principles and Practices* (New York: HarperCollins, 1990).
13. Ibid., 44.
14. https://recruitloop.com/blog/zappos-hiring-for-culture-and-the-bizarre-things-they-do/
15. Kim Scott, *Radical Candor: Be a Kick-Ass Boss Without Losing Your Humanity* (New York: St. Martin's Press, 2017), 8.
16. Ibid., 9.
17. Ibid.
18. www.recode.net/2017/4/13/15295070/transcript-kim-scott-book-radical-candor-live-onstage-recode-decode

9. Vocational Courage for Organizations

1. www.wired.com/2000/04/ben-jerrys-sells-out/
2. Ibid.
3. www.benjerry.com/whats-new/2016/38-birthday-fun-facts
4. www.statista.com/statistics/190426/top-ice-cream-brands-in-the-united-states/
5. www.washingtonpost.com/business/on-small-business/when-we-were-small-ben-and-jerrys/2014/05/14/069b6cae-dac4-11e3-8009-71de85b9c527_story.html?utm_term=.fba8839b7815
6. Ibid.
7. Ibid.
8. www.benjerry.com/values

9. www.benjerry.com/about-us/how-were-structured#3timeline
10. Ibid.
11. www.thebalancecareers.com/biglaw-nickname-definition-2164198
12. www2.deloitte.com/global/en/pages/about-deloitte/articles/millennial-survey-making-impact-through-employers.html
13. www.lovellcorporation.com/wp-content/uploads/2017/11/The2017ChangeGenerationReport-Lovell.pdf
14. Ibid.
15. www.thewaltdisneycompany.com/about/
16. https://help-en-us.nike.com/app/answer/a_id/113
17. http://s2.q4cdn.com/056532643/files/doc_financials/2018/annual/WMT-2018_Annual-Report.pdf
18. https://arstechnica.com/gadgets/2011/08/tim-cook-e-mail-to-apple-employees-apple-is-not-going-to-change/
19. Jim Collins, Foreword for *Hesselbein on Leadership* (San Francisco: Jossey-Bass. 2002).
20. www.patagonia.com/company-history.html
21. www.inc.com/magazine/201303/liz-welch/the-way-i-work-yvon-chouinard-patagonia.html
22. www.patagonia.com/company-info.html

Afterword: The Contagion of Courage

1. www.pwc.com/us/en/about-us/corporate-responsibility/assets/pwc-putting-purpose-to-work-purpose-survey-report.pdf